GW00480487

In a personal, warm and invites "the people called denomination age — th.. revisit, rediscover and reimagine the "why" of Methodism... Focusing less upon strategies and initiatives and more about both an openness to the reawakening of the Holy Spirit and a renewed confidence in God's mandate to the Church, he urges us with some passion to remember our past and in so doing, find afresh our future in God. This book is a timely and timeless reminder that I hope will be read widely throughout British Methodism and beyond.

Revd Dr Martyn Atkins, Former General Secretary of the Methodist Church in Britain, President of the Methodist Conference, 2007/8

How can our origin story help us reimagine and reshape our future story? In this gem of a book, Leslie Newton begs the question, could the crisis of institutional decline be an opportunity for the people called Methodists to experience a death and resurrection of sorts? His answer is a resounding and hopeful yes! Newton offers insight into how the fresh expressions movement helps recover the core why and missional practices of early Methodism. This could be the very gift our hurting world needs. A form of Methodism that gives itself away with Godly zeal for the renewal of the church and nations, to spread scriptural holiness across the land. This book is foundational reading for any person or organization seeking to cultivate a blended ecology of church.

Michael Beck (michaeladambeck.com) is Director of the Fresh Expressions House of Studies at United Theological Seminary and Director of Fresh Expressions for The United Methodist Church. He is the author of nine books, and considered a leading voice in the Fresh Expressions movement.

Wesley's final words were, "Best of all, God is with us." As the Church tackles decline, Leslie wants to discover God's best for us now.
Revd Graham Thompson, President of the Methodist Conference, 2022-23

Leslie helpfully articulates Methodism's raison d'être as being rooted in Wesley's divine missional call to "spread scriptural holiness" through "love in action." Amen to that!
Karen Openshaw, Former board member Fresh Expressions Ltd

This book cries out to me! Why? Because it is filled with passion, grace, holiness, generosity and the call to give it all away: the keys to revival and transformation.
Major Andrew Vertigan, The Salvation Army's Territorial Pioneer and Fresh Expressions Mission Enabler

Leslie writes an inspiring, compelling account of why a rejuvenated Methodism can revive us. With passion, grace and clarity, he conveys great hope for the future.
Dr Nigel Pimlott, coach, consultant, analyst and activist

Rooted in God's gracious activity, here's a renewed vision for the twenty-first century. This is a hope-filled invitation to rediscover the richness and vibrancy of the early Methodist movement.
Deacon Eunice Attwood, Church at the Margins Officer, Methodist Church

REVIVE
US AGAIN

*Rejuvenating a movement
of transformation*

PublishU Ltd

www.PublishU.com

Thanks

With thanks to the Methodist Church and in particular the Yorkshire North and East District, for the gift and space of a three-month sabbatical in 2021 which provided the opportunity to begin to study and write what has now become this book.

Heartfelt thanks also to Peter Goodman for his encouraging and incisive reviews and comments at various stages of my book-writing.

Finally, and most deeply, I am grateful to my wife, Gill, and daughter, Laura, for their unfailing encouragement, support and patience throughout this process.

Contents

LESLIE NEWTON

Preface

Every seven years, the Methodist Church generously offers its ministers a sabbatical: a three-month gift of space. Each minister can decide, with appropriate support and guidance, how that time is used. I chose to focus my sabbatical of 2021 on exploring more deeply than I had previously, how the early Methodist movement took root and grew so rapidly and effectively.

I found the research both illuminating and inspiring. It stirred my heart in ways that I had not anticipated as I looked at "what was" and began to dream of "what could be" in the twenty-first century.

This book is the fruit of my reading and reflections. I have presented much of this in two study days within the Yorkshire North and East District where I currently serve as District Chair. I have also presented a shorter version twice online. I was encouraged to write this book by some who attended.

I also spent sabbatical time looking at some of Charles Wesley's hymns and, in particular, some that I'd never really engaged with before. My hunch is that this is mainly because the set tunes had never inspired, so the words had remained overlooked! One of these in particular took a hold of me:

Singing the Faith 490, "Being of Beings, God of Love"

Being of beings, God of love,
to You our hearts we raise:
Your all-sustaining power we prove,
and gladly sing Your praise.

Yours, wholly Yours, we long to be:
our sacrifice receive;
made, and preserved, and then set free,
to You ourselves we give.

Heavenward our every wish aspires;
for all Your mercies' store,
the sole return Your love requires
is that we ask for more.

For more we ask; we open then
our hearts to embrace Your will;
turn, and revive us, Lord, again,
with all Your fullness fill.

Come, Holy Ghost, the Saviour's love
shed in our hearts abroad;
so shall we ever live, and move,
and be with Christ in God.

I was so moved by these words that I composed a new tune, hoping to give them fresh and appropriate life. I particularly appreciate Wesley's insight, in verse three, that the sole return God wants for offering His love to us, is that we ask for more![1]

Also of significance is the prayer in verse four: "Revive us, Lord, again" (a quote from Psalm 85:6.) That line became so important to me as I continued through my sabbatical and during the writing of this book: the confident prayer that God might still revive us for these days, just as He offered His life-giving and life-shaping love to the birth of the Methodist movement.

Whilst explaining the title of this book, I've opted to choose the word "rejuvenate" in the subtitle (instead of, for instance, "re-awaken") because of how fitting its dictionary definition seems to be: "to restore to youthful vigour," "to make fresh or new again," or, from its root in physical geography, "to restore a river to a condition characteristic of a younger landscape."

So, I hope that this very personal exploration of what has become deeply significant to me about our roots and our potential, will be of interest. I dare to hope that it might inspire wider conversation about our future. My prayer will continue to be that "the people called Methodists" will recover a life-transforming openness to the riches of God's grace, that God might indeed revive us and that thereby we might be rejuvenated as a movement of spiritual and social transformation.

Leslie Newton, June 2023

I am daring to ask and pray that we might devote ourselves to being re-awakened by God's Spirit in our collective Methodist heart, mind and soul.

Chapter 1

Time to Recover Our Buried Treasure

Me, and "The people called Methodists"

I owe so very much to the Methodist Church. It has held, nurtured and shaped so much of my life. Throughout my childhood and youth, "the people called Methodists"[2] have provided a place beyond the home that always felt like home.

They have provided the source of some of my best friendships. They have encouraged me to "find my feet" in music, in youth work, in leadership and then in preaching. They have patiently held me through my journey from "belonging" to "believing": of gradually developing a personal faith and then making it my own.

It was within Methodism that I found the most wonderful wife and it has nurtured the spiritual and social life of our precious daughter. It welcomed me into its presbyteral ministry and has supported me as I have exercised that ministry in Barnsley, Bramhall, York and now as Chair of District in Yorkshire North and East.

It is little surprise then that I carry a deep loyalty and a love for Methodism, embedded so deeply within the story of my life as it is. It is in so many ways "home" to me.

Facing Reality

It is all the more painful, therefore, to have to fully recognise and admit the reality of the baked-in, inexorable and consistent decline in Methodism's size, influence and reach over many decades.

Of course I quickly add that the landscape is not universally bleak. There are still many committed, passionate and faithful people. I can happily point to Methodist churches that are healthy and thriving; to committed, inspired and fruitful work that is truly making a Kingdom difference.

However, there can be no disputing that, by every reasonable indicator, our church generally is on a sustained and consistent path of becoming smaller and older, with a less dynamic presence within the communities of our land.

We are, of course, by no means unique in being in this position. It is a feature of most mainstream denominations within our country. The context and reasons for this are widely explored in theological writing. The significant Methodist Statement, "Called to Love and Praise," written in 1999, recognised in one of its concluding passages: "This Statement has been written at a time uncongenial in many ways to the life and growth of the Churches of Western Europe. They face a time of rapid change in cultures which are profoundly individualistic, secular and materialistic."[3]

Whether those external reasons for "uncongeniality" are the primary and, therefore, unavoidable grounds for continuing decline is something for contention within this book.

As a counterpoint to lamenting our consistent contraction, I need also to affirm that there are, of course, theologically rich arguments to remind us that small is very often beautiful and that there is great beauty, life and potential in small things. Not least, we see this reminder springing out from many of the parables of Jesus and the birth and development of the early church. It is certainly the case that we need to value the small highly as not just a sign of the Kingdom of God, but a home to the Kingdom of God being authentically established.

It is also important to observe at the outset that "the people called Methodists" have by no means been passive in seeking to respond to our deep-set decline. We have developed and embraced many schemes and initiatives to try to encourage our renewal over the years. Indeed, there is a danger that we have sometimes succumbed to "initiative-itis" as one scheme or form of reorganisation has quickly succeeded another.

That has all added, for some at least, to the institutional weariness. I won't labour that here, as it has been entirely and thoroughly well-intentioned and faithful in hope and ambition. I am absolutely not setting out to present a commentary of criticism and most certainly not beyond any which reflects on my own efforts along the way.

But God is Not Finished with Us Yet

However, I want to press the case for us, "the people called Methodists," to once again be galvanised and motivated by our "divinely appointed mission" that has at its heart a call to "spread scriptural holiness through the land."

John Wesley famously wrote in 1786 in his "Thoughts on Methodism": "I am not afraid that the people called Methodists should ever cease to exist either in Europe or America. But I am afraid lest they should only exist as a dead sect, having the form of religion without power. And this undoubtedly will be the case, unless they hold fast to the doctrine, spirit and discipline with which they first set out."

Over 230 years on, these words continue to offer an urgent challenge: is the systemic decline of Methodism in Britain a sign of "time up?"

I really don't believe so. Indeed, I echo the affirmation of Past President of the Methodist Conference, Kenneth Howcroft within his Presidential Address to the Conference in 2014: "But God has not finished with us yet!"[4]

Instead, I believe God is calling us to re-discover confidence in our sacred and particular mandate, to re-discover our true clothes and play our distinctive part in the great richness of the "one holy, catholic and apostolic church."

We surely still have a part to play in God's great mission!

One of the reasons that encourages my continuing confidence for the future is the great synergy I see between Methodism's founding roots and motivations and the momentum of the Fresh Expressions movement as it burgeons today. How profoundly and deeply that movement echoes with the principles that underpinned the early growth of "the people called Methodists." There is such amazing potential for us to play a distinctive, crucial and transformative part in God's renewing mission.

I am deeply encouraged, excited and filled with hope that within God's heart and providence there is still a valuable contribution that "the people called Methodists" can make in these lands.

My Cri de Coeur

So, in what follows, I am attempting to build a case that there are some particular charisms and motivations at the heart of Methodism which remain distinctive and valuable, despite them having been overlooked and practically neglected for many years. By their re-discovery and re-imagination, I believe we can again contribute something enriching and of great potential to the wider church of which we are fully and wholly a part.

They are rooted in and emerge from (as is the case with most organisations or movements) the early founding years. Encouragingly, much still lies embedded in our very DNA: deeply within the "coding" of contemporary Methodism.[5] Sadly, as I say, they remain undervalued and overlooked in a good deal of our Connexional life. I therefore recognise that at least some of what I set out here feels to be going against the contemporary, mainstream direction of travel. That's a personal challenge for me. However, nonetheless, I seek to set out my heart here as plainly and winsomely as I can.

Here, then, is my ard de coeur, that "the people called Methodists" have an urgent and compelling "reason for being" for the twenty-first century. What we have to offer is an important and distinctive contribution to fulfilling God's mission. It is by treasuring our distinctiveness and focusing on these things passionately that we can contribute most effectively to the wider church.

I am not setting out here a new programme or strategy. Quite the opposite. I am daring to ask and pray that we might devote ourselves to being re-awakened by God's Spirit in our collective Methodist heart, mind and soul.

I will press the case for us to seek a renewing of our church humbly and yet boldly as a movement that takes seriously once again the charisms and distinctive qualities that lie at the heart of our DNA: that sees the huge needs of people and the world and, in embodying God's compassion and grace, we play our part in contributing to spiritual and social transformation.

Two founding reasons stir me on: firstly – and most importantly – my faith in God. God has not given up on His world! Secondly – and significantly – because amidst our enduring decline, Methodism is still full of faith-filled people who love God and love each other and the world.

Yes, we face some commonly-shared frustrations, perhaps most notably that we have become so calcified and restricted by the stuff of institutionalism that we feel entrapped. As my friend, Simon Pringle (Methodist and Honorary Professor at University of Edinburgh Business School) reflects about the dangers for institutions, "they become better at doing what used to be important!" To appropriate the heart-warming sentiment from Charles

Wesley's anthemic hymn, I long for Methodism's chains to fall off and our heart to be freed once again!

Despite all that causes us anxiety, we have, I believe, a shared desire: for Methodism to once again journey towards fulfilling its world-changing potential.

And I say this, ultimately and crucially, not because I love the Methodist Church and owe it so much but because God so loves the world! In these post-modern, post-Christendom, post-almost everything days, there are signs that God is enabling what is being referred to as a "new reformation." As Leonard Sweet, American theologian and author, is quoted as saying: "What the Spirit is up to in the new reformation is not about making a better church, but making a better world."[6]

This lies at the very core of my heart as I write this book.

Could it be, to quote Sweet again, that it is high time for "the people called Methodists" to show some originality? "In its truest sense, originality means a return to origins or a rediscovery of one's roots – not merely to reproduce the current original, which is self-extinction, but to recapitulate the original in the current context, a fresh choreography for daily life of an old dance."[7]

Remembering our "why" can be our tuning fork, our rallying cry, our clarion call to renewed prayer, expectant waiting on God and purposeful pursuit of mission and discipleship.

Chapter 2

Renewing Confidence in our "Why"

Start with Why

Every organisation needs to be clear about its identity and purpose: why it exists. That is often (though not always!) clear at the outset. However, ensuring that the essential "why we exist" is not forgotten as time moves on is vital for long-term success. It is all too easy for the "why" to become blurred, diluted and forgotten as movements transition into organisations and institutions. Other priorities compete for attention and resources. Many of these priorities can be attractively good and honourable in themselves and yet they carry with them the danger of shifting energy and momentum away from the founding "why."

This is a challenge that all organisations and institutions have to face as they mature and God's people are not exempt. Remember the Israelites wandering in the wilderness struggling so often to remember the "why" of leaving captivity to flourish in the Promised Land?

American author and speaker, Simon Sinek, recognises this forcefully in his best-selling book "Start with Why." He is clear that organisations only thrive through having a compelling clarity of purpose – they know their "why": "Your WHY is your central belief. It's the concept that motivates you to get out of bed in the morning. In terms of an organisation, it's the reason you're in business."[8]

So it is for "the people called Methodists." A shared and compelling understanding of who we are and why we exist is fundamental in galvanising unity and releasing energy. A compelling "why" underpins and releases zeal, enthusiasm and passion. It also crucially prevents 'not the main things' from gradually becoming 'the main thing.'

As we chart our way through the twenty-first century, "the people called Methodists" need to rediscover that clarity. Not just why we used to exist but why, for God, we exist here and now. Could we be suffering from collective amnesia?

Remembering our "why" can be our tuning fork, our rallying cry, our clarion call to renewed prayer, expectant waiting on God and purposeful pursuit of mission and discipleship. Once it is confidently restored, I believe that hearts will be stirred, minds enlivened, hands and feet active; all our being responding with fresh clarity and renewed passion.

As Sinek mentions, organisations often find it easier to rather articulate their "what" or their "how." Perhaps the same can be seen within the Methodist Church in recent years. There has been some excellent and helpful thinking about priorities and the way ahead. "Our Calling" produced in 2000[9], and then re-affirmed in 2018, sets out a framework for how to be the church. A reaffirming "Our Calling" report in 2018 goes on to reference Standing Orders and a WCC statement.[10]

The report goes on to set out priority areas for focus and attention[11] and are set out in the context of responding to and re-affirming "Our Calling":

- To make more followers of Jesus Christ through mission and evangelism;

- To help members deepen their faith and to put their faith into action (discipleship);

- To find ways to support the improvement in the quality of worship offered to God;

- To support the development of district and circuit mission plans;

- To grow the number, variety and breadth of vocations;

- To develop the property of the Church to support mission and evangelism;

- To be a more inclusive and welcoming Church;

- To evaluate and revise decision making processes of the Church so that they are effective and efficient enabling the Church to pursue its commitment to mission;

- To enable the Church to be a good neighbour, especially to people in need and to be prophetic and to challenge injustice;

- To ensure the Church fulfils its regulatory and good oversight responsibilities in key areas.

All of this is doing excellent work in identifying the answers to "what" and "how" questions.

But what about our "why?" Why should the Methodist Church continue to exist? Amongst a whole range of historic denominations and emerging church networks of many different flavours and shades, what is the compelling "why" of "the people called Methodists?"

Discovering the Tradition behind the Traditions

Sinek goes on to note that so often the answer to this is found by attending deeply to our DNA and our earliest days. "Our why comes from looking back."[12] And, of course, that thought should be no surprise or novelty to us as Christians; as people who are called to remember our place in the great unfolding story of God's heart and mission.

In Isaiah 43:16-19 we read: "This is what the Lord says – He who made a way through the sea, a path through the mighty waters, who drew out the chariots and horses, the army and reinforcements together, and then lay there, never to rise again, extinguished, snuffed out like a wick; Forget the former things; do not dwell on the past. See, I am doing a new thing! Now it springs up; do you not perceive it?"

This text deserves careful reflection. We read that God is doing something new. However, crucially, before that declaration of the new, comes the recapitulation of God's nature and all that has gone before. The new is rooted in a recognition of the old. The "why" of the future is cast upon the "why" of the old.

Sinek puts it like this: **"The** WHY does not come from looking ahead at what you want to achieve and figuring out an appropriate strategy to get there. It is not borne out of market research. It does not come from extensive interviews with customers or even employees. It comes from looking in the completely opposite direction from where you are now. Finding WHY is a process of discovery, not invention ... The hard part is the discipline to trust one's gut, to stay true to one's purpose, cause or beliefs. Remaining completely in balance and authentic is the most difficult part."[13]

So, again, why has God called us to be "the people called Methodists?" What is our distinctive and unique nature and being? How do we answer that in such a way that our minds are racing, our hearts are beating faster and we are increasingly ready to offer our lives, as Romans 12:1 has it, as 'living sacrifices?'

This question forces us to look, as American Methodist, Elaine Heath, puts it so helpfully, to see "the tradition behind the traditions."[14]

As we look back, we can see that the why of "the people called Methodists" became increasingly clear through the journey of the formative years of John Wesley's childhood, early adulthood, ordination within the Church of England and subsequent Aldersgate Street experience. As the nascent Methodism took shape under his guiding and pioneering leadership, so the sense of calling and purpose came strongly from his lead. He embodied the essence of what the developing movement was all about (as we will further explore later in this book).

We find the earliest and clearest response to the question "Why Methodism?" given by John Wesley at the 1763 Methodist Conference: "What may we reasonably believe to be God's purpose in raising up preachers called Methodist? To reform the nation and, in particular, the Church; to spread scriptural holiness over the land."

As we look through the fragmented history of "the people called Methodists" since then, we see, time and time again, affirmation of this "why." The Liverpool Conference of 1820, which was shocked into heartfelt reflection by a first fall in numbers, re-affirmed its commitment to the why: "Let us afresh, solemnly and heartily recognise the original purpose of Methodism, 'to spread Scriptural holiness through the land' and ever regard this as the first and great calling of the Methodist people, and especially of the Preachers."[15]

When the Wesleyan and Primitive branches of the Methodist family came together in 1932, this affirmation of the why was embodied within the Deed of Union: "The Methodist Church claims and cherishes its place in the Holy Catholic Church which is the Body of Christ. It rejoices in the inheritance of the apostolic faith and loyally accepts the fundamental principles of the historic creeds and of the Protestant Reformation. It ever remembers that in the providence of God Methodism was raised up to spread scriptural holiness through the land by the proclamation of the evangelical faith and declares its unfaltering resolve to be true to its divinely appointed mission."[16]

Do pause to reflect on the powerful resolve expressed here! Our "why" described as our "divinely appointed mission" to be pursued with "unfaltering resolve."

When a major reorganisation of trusteeship took place in 1976, the consequential Methodist Church Act could have stepped away from this but did not.

Interestingly in 2013, in the midst of long-running conversations about closer relationship with the Church of England, a report of the Joint Implementation Commission said this: "Methodism has always seen its reason for existence as being mission. In the words of the Deed of Union of the Methodist Church of Great Britain: 'It ever remembers that in the providence of God Methodism was raised up to spread scriptural holiness through the land by the proclamation of the evangelical faith and declares its unfaltering resolve to be true to its divinely appointed mission.' Theoretically at least it has seen the way it is structured as being contingent on achieving that end."[17]

"Theoretically at least": what an honest and interesting admission!

So Here is the Compelling Why!

"Spreading scriptural holiness over the land, reforming the nation and in particular the church."

Here is our movement's distinctive cornerstone, laid with some clarity way back in 1763. This "why" shaped and gave energy to the movement in its early days and it has, when push comes to shove, been used as a uniting motif ever since.

And yet it has also been hiding in plain sight! A quick internet search shows that many Methodist churches, circuits and even the connexional website quote these phrases as foundational. And then so often the words are simply left hanging there – in splendid isolation as it were – bearing little impact on what else follows and with no significant unpacking and exploration. They remain unreferred to, the subsequent 'what' and 'how' at least semi-detached.

As Sweet so starkly puts it: "Methodism needs to be re-introduced to its true self. We've been more caught up in the drama of self-narration than the transmission of gospel-narration. Methodist has lost its true representation ... We aren't singing our song. We aren't living our own story."[18]

Instead, our why should be like a huge church bell pealing its evocative call consistently and emphatically. But it feels like the clapper has been lost!

Howcroft, in his Presidential Address of 2014, pointed to this concern. As I have done, he affirms these words as representing "still the basis of our Church, our Conference, our Methodist Connexion." But then he asked these important questions: "Yet do we still ever remember what it says? Do we know what our 'divinely appointed mission' is? And do we still have an unfaltering resolve to be true to it?"[19]

Now of course, there is substantial unpacking of all this to be done – perhaps particularly for our contemporary ears.

Ironically, perhaps, there is more work to do because our why has effectively been neglected for so long. That is what I hope to begin to do in this book. I will offer some thoughts here but there will be more that could and should be added. Significant reflection and further work is desperately needed to re-appropriate with confidence our fullest appreciation of our why for the twenty-first century, to rejuvenate the heart-warming focus of mission which can shape lives and the very heart of our movement.

Let me close this chapter by repeating those amazing keynote words within our 1932 Deed of Union — words which surely must challenge and invite us more deeply to explore our why: "the Methodist Church declares its unfaltering resolve to be true to its divinely appointed mission." Wow!

Could it be that a recovery of this commitment and passion might help revitalise "the people called Methodists" for a new and fruitful season of mission? As Sweet so marvellously dreams: "I believe God's clock keeps perfect time. I believe God may have raised up John Wesley as much for the twenty-first century as for the eighteenth century ... I believe that even though what we now call Methodism is in too many ways what Wesley came to get rid of it, it need not come to this. Sometimes our solutions lie as much in the past as in the present or the future ... I believe what historians call the 'Methodist Revolution' is an unfinished revolution."[20]

A first step in renewing confidence in our distinctive "why" as "the people called Methodists" is for us to be rejuvenated through our passionate celebration of the Good News of Jesus.

Chapter 3

On Fire with the Gospel

Almost a century ago, WE Sangster, influential Methodist minister, wrote: "Methodism can be born again."[21] In many ways (sadly) it feels like a very contemporary read. Many of his concerns then are exactly those that burden us today. He uses a humorous but telling illustration to highlight the importance of "the people called Methodists" having clarity about, and confidence in, our why. He tells of a man who "went into a restaurant and ordered lunch. When the waiter brought the soup it was a poor, colourless and uninviting liquid and tasted no better than it looked. So the hungry fellow called the waiter back. 'Waiter, he asked, 'what soup is this?' 'No particular soup, sir,' said the waiter. 'Just soup.' 'Ah,' said the diner, as he gazed on the watery scene. 'I see. And only just!'"[22]

Sangster tells this story not to press a case against closer ecumenical relationships – or for reunion with the Church of England. No, actually, quite the opposite. He longs for Methodism – and every denomination and church network – to bring their distinctiveness to the table. We "can cherish, as a dear possession, those facets of truth which God gave to [our] branch of the Church and bear it forward as a definite part of the whole glory which is yet to be revealed, seeking, in a spirit of charity, to understand what others have found precious in their communion, but not forgetting, as a good steward, that [we] have something to give as well as to gain."[23]

In galvanising ourselves around our founding "why" – our "sacred mandate" – and our "divinely appointed mission," it is essential that we recognise, inhabit and focus our life on the distinctive charisms of our movement. To re-quote Elaine Heath: we need to rediscover the "tradition behind the traditions."

So, a first step in renewing confidence in our distinctive "why" as "the people called Methodists" is for us to be rejuvenated through our passionate celebration of the Good News of Jesus. In Ephesians 3:18-19 we read: "I pray that you may have the power to comprehend, with all the saints, what is the breadth and length and height and depth, and to know the love of Christ that surpasses knowledge, so that you may be filled with all the fullness of God." It is that kind of heartfelt desire that we need to prayerfully and devotedly seek after as we recover the distinctive God-given mandate given to us.

Captivated by the Astonishingly Good News of the Gospel

Our starting point is surely to stand in awe at the extraordinary love of God. How deeply the world needs to know and discover the inexhaustible and comprehensive riches of God: the God who brought creation out of chaos, who breathes life into every person; the God who has loved us from the start of time and the God who can't possibly love us more than now and will never love us less; the God who saves us from ourselves and who wants to assure us that sin does not have the first word and needn't have the last word; the God who longs for us to have an assurance of our eternal flourishing and would rather die than live without us; the God who wants to fill our lives with His presence and enable us to discover life in all its fullness.

"Called to Love and Praise," the significant Methodist Conference Statement of 1999 exploring the nature of the Church, expresses these truths more formally like this:

"At the heart of this Gospel is the revelation that God, as Father, Son and Holy Spirit, embraces the world, each member of the human race, and every living creature, with a love which not only creates, but re-creates and heals in the face of humankind's tragic, self-centred fragmentation. This is God's 'mission' to the world: God does not exist in isolation or detachment from creation, but with the passionate care of a father or mother engages with it, inviting humankind to find its lasting centre and home in the divine love. This love is the ultimate, inescapable centre and framework of all things. For this reason the Bible bears witness to the 'Kingdom' of God, for God reigns, in spite of the dark abysses of human history, suffering and even death. The climax to the Biblical testimony to both the mission and kingdom of God is the crucifixion and resurrection of Jesus – God's ultimate act of solidarity with and sacrifice for the world and God's definitive victory over evil. Out of this Gospel, the Church gladly acknowledges its vocation to celebrate the love of God in its worship, to share his life in its fellowship, and to be the agent of His generosity and compassion in a needy world."[24]

God promises a new heaven and earth and in Jesus, He invites us to full commitment in prayer and daily living to seeing God's kingdom come on earth as it is in heaven.

All this, of course, is the treasure beyond measure that Wesley began to value with fresh insight after his heart-warming moment at Aldersgate Street in 1738.

Responding to a Seeking and Sending God

Distinctively (but not uniquely), the early Wesley-an movement brought to life this life-changing appreciation of God's heart and mission by recognising God as both "seeking" and "sending." As American Methodist Michael Beck puts it: "John Wesley experienced God as a seeking and sending God, whose essential nature is love. This mindset fuelled his actions."[25]

So, our why is built upon the affirmation that God seeks every single one of us out: a seeking that pours out of the perfect, self-sacrificial love seen most completely in Jesus. Then, just as God is a seeking God, He calls us to share in the seeking as He sends us out. So it was that as John Wesley's life was transformed by the life-changing reality of this seeking love, he became able to embrace, albeit reluctantly, field preaching.

It was in 1739 that he was persuaded by evangelist George Whitfield to preach in the open air. He wrote in his journal: "I could scarce reconcile myself at first to this strange way of preaching in the fields..."

It is worth noting that as Wesley, of course, an Anglican Priest, stepped from pulpit to field there were many quick to criticise. The whole concept of field preaching was anathema to their understanding of models of church which were primarily attractional. In resolute defence Wesley wrote: "Will you say (as I have known some tender-hearted Christians), 'Then it is their own fault?' And so it was my fault and yours when we went astray like sheep that were lost. Yet the Shepherd of souls sought after us and went after us in the wilderness. And 'oughtest not thou to have compassion on thy fellow servants, as He had pity on thee?' Ought we not also 'to seek,' as far as in us lies, 'and to save that which is lost?'"[26]

So, God is a "seeking God" and also a "sending God." The sending flows directly from our personal experience of a seeking God. Sweet notes "heart warmed" and the "world is my parish" as these two sides of the coin: "The essence of Methodism's genius resides in two famous Wesleyan mantras: 'heart strangely warmed' and 'the world is our parish.' For Wesley, internal combustion, the former, led to external combustion, the latter."[27]

As Beck puts it, we should "continue to emphasise a personal experience of a seeking and sending trinitarian God, whose primary characteristic is relentless love."[28]

It is important to recognise the Wesley-an distinctiveness of being, inherently, a 'sent,' rather than a 'called' people. We see this, for instance, in the way our Methodist history features itinerancy so strongly: being a people on the move.

So, one of the ways in which Wesley sought to renew the church was to move away from what had become a largely attractional-only form of church, at its worst passively there waiting to see if people might come to join their ranks. Wesley recognised that this missed the vital essence of God's mission — that of seeking and sending.

Here is something rich and precious for us to recover about God's heart and mission: God is firstly a seeking God. But then God sends us out to share that love with the same passion by which we were sought! As God in Jesus came and moved into our neighbourhood, to seek and save that which is lost (Luke 19:10), so He also came to send His followers out, filled with His Spirit (John 20:21).

Whilst by no means being unique to "the people called Methodists," it does lie at the heart of understanding our why. The Methodist movement rose up with this at its heart. It began to play its part in renewing and revitalising God's church by embodying boldly both the seeking and sending nature of God.

This is God's mission: from a heart so full of perfect love God reaches out to us, and invites us to join in with His mission. This starts to frame for us what we mean by "spreading scriptural holiness."

REVIVE US AGAIN

In the multi-faceted, complex and hugely variegated twenty-first century our Methodist calling is a mandate to reach: every home and heart, every neighbourhood and network, every community and culture, across every inch of our land and of cyberspace.

Chapter 4

A Passion for Holiness

We have already seen that holiness has an absolutely fundamental and foundational place at the heart of appreciating the why. How sad – and consequential – it is, then, that we seem to have become so uncomfortable and ill at ease in our use of that word. Holiness has become a neglected and almost practically redundant concept to many Methodists. As Wesleyan Academic, Philip Meadows, starkly puts it: "For many the very word 'holiness' is enough to strike fear into the hearts. Over the years, we have done much to make it appear either unattractive or unattainable."[29]

If we are really to rediscover the heartbeat of our "divinely appointed mission", it must surely include, therefore, an urgent recovery of our appreciation of the "beauty of holiness."

Calvin Samuel, British Methodist Minister, enthusiastically quotes Ruth Etchells, former Principal of St John's College, Durham University, who described holiness like this: "Holiness is actually the shining dazzle of profoundest divine love exchanged continually with the Trinity and poured out for creation in all its forms for our deepest and most joyful good."[30]

Samuel then helpfully elaborates on this quote: "First, that holiness is a shining dazzle. Too few people are inclined to think of holiness as *shiny*. Most of us think of holiness as dour, hard work, sober and serious. Etchells reminds us that holiness is *attractive*. Second, that holiness is rooted in divine *love*. This not only reminds us that holiness and love are necessarily linked but also that holiness is the core of God's being. If holiness is rooted in divine love, and God is Love, then, whenever we talk about holiness, we are in fact trying to describe that which is the very heart of God. Third, holiness is rooted in divine action. Holiness is divine love poured out on creation. Who does this pouring out? God. Why is the love poured out? For our deepest and most joyful good. Holiness is rooted in the gracious action of God."[31]

It is this attractive and positive understanding of holiness that had centre stage in early Methodism. It is this compelling and appealing appreciation of holiness which lies at the heart of our mobilising why and that so urgently needs to be rediscovered. It is summarised so winsomely by John Wesley himself in the phrase: "Holiness is love in action."[32]

As I noted earlier, despite its current lack of attention within contemporary Methodism, plenty has been written through the years with a view to exploring more deeply an understanding and appreciation of holiness. I only begin to scratch the surface here. But even in doing that, I hope that we might together begin to renew, at least, our appreciation that here is something remarkably rich and powerful – too valuable for us to lose sight of, a treasure for the wider church and most importantly for the world we are called to love and serve.

Firstly, we can be clear in affirming, as Howcroft argues, that holiness should not be thought of as being a withdrawal or separation from the world. It is, he reminds us, quite the opposite and is about deep engagement with the world as we are transformed in the love of God.

Howcroft quotes Wesley as affirming that scriptural holiness is no less than the image of God stamped upon the heart; it is none other than the whole mind which was in Christ Jesus. That "involves all of what we would call our instincts, feelings, emotional dispositions, ways of thinking and spiritual sensitivities being brought together, made whole and made holy. It makes us respond to God thankfully and lovingly in turn. And, says Wesley, if we start to love God, we shall naturally end up loving the rest of the world as well. We will not be able to help it. God's love will not let us."[33]

Heath also emphasises this theme as she longs, like me, for a Methodist Church renewed in its divinely appointed mission: "The Church is called Holy, wrote John Wesley, because it is holy. This need not be a cloistered holiness, but it is intentional and communal – a holiness in the midst of the stresses and strains of everyday life. If we can recover that, we will recover a church that is vital and effective in the twenty-first century."[34]

"Called to Love and Praise" confirms this practical nature of holiness as being part and parcel of what should be our Methodist self-understanding: "Wesley's call to personal faith and to holiness reflected a concern for justice and integrity in everyday life, and also an optimism about what the grace of God could accomplish in human lives. Members of the societies were committed to a common discipline of Christian life, gave each other support, and acted as a task force for the Church in witness and social action. They resembled a religious order, with their annual Conference acting like a 'chapter' for the itinerant 'order of preachers.' Like the friars of St. Francis in an earlier age, Wesley's movement found ways to 'fill the gaps' at a time when the old parish system was failing to keep up with rapid population growth in Britain's new industrial areas."[35]

American Methodist, Henry Knight, puts it like this: "Holiness of heart and life, centred on love for God and neighbour, was the orienting goal of the mission. The polity of the Methodist movement was never an end in itself, but was always intended to serve the mission. The [Book of] Discipline, classes and bands, itinerant preachers, [connexion], and conference were all designed to enable the movement to fulfil its purpose of renewing lives, the church, and the nation."[36]

The Breadth and Depth of Holiness

So, firstly, let us be clear about the rich and comprehensive scope of holiness: our mandate is nothing less than to be reaching out to the heart of every individual and to be playing our part in the transformation of the land.

Our mandate to spread scriptural holiness through the land is utterly comprehensive. As I dared to say to the Methodist Conference a few years ago: "in the multi-faceted, complex and hugely variegated twenty-first century our Methodist calling is a mandate to reach:

- every home and heart

- every neighbourhood and network

- every community and culture

- across every inch of our land and of cyberspace."

Heath puts it like this as she looked at early Methodism: "a holiness movement that evangelised people both inside and outside the Church ... Methodism was a holiness movement that initiated people into a holy life, revealed in Jesus Christ, anchored in the Church, empowered by the Holy Spirit, surrendered to the reign of God, for the transformation of the world."[37]

To help us explore the breadth and depth of holiness, it is helpful and important to look at the key foundational Wesley-an dimensions of holiness deeply rooted within our history: "personal holiness," "social holiness" and then that core phrase lying at the heart of our why: "scriptural holiness."

Personal Holiness

As we noted in the last chapter, the very nature of God's love is to seek out every single person, enabling the heart to be warmed, offering an experience of "new birth" and declaring liberating forgiveness. Wesley's sermons are rich sources of inspiration and encouragement here.

But for now, may these brief words inspire us afresh: Wesley was asked, "Who is a Methodist, according to your own account?" He answered, "A Methodist is one who has the love of God shed abroad in his (sic) heart by the Holy Ghost given unto him; one who loves the Lord his God with all his heart, with all his soul, with all his mind and with all his strength."[38]

Wesley also identified tho "marks of a true Methodist": "He (sic) is a Christian not in name only, but in heart and in life. He is inwardly and outwardly conformed to the will of God, as revealed in the written Word. He thinks, speaks and lives according to the 'method' laid down in the revelation of Jesus Christ. His soul is 'renewed after the image of God in righteousness and in all true holiness.' And 'having the mind that was in Christ,' he 'so walks as Christ also walked.' ... God is the joy of his heart, and the desire of his soul ... He is therefore happy in God ... as having in him a well of water springing up into everlasting life and overflowing his soul with peace and joy."[39]

As Past President of the Methodist Conference, Richard Teal, writes: "For Wesley, evangelical conversion was just the beginning of the Christian journey. All that God has done for us in Jesus Christ paves the way for the work of the Holy Spirit in our hearts, to transform our lives totally. Holiness or perfection is about spiritual maturity. Donald English, Methodist Minister, used to say that the Methodist people 'want to be better than they are' and by that he meant that Methodist Christians yearn and desire to be better disciples of Jesus Christ than they are. This yearning is a pursuit of holiness or perfect love."[40]

Social Holiness

It is hugely significant that Wesley recognised that personal holiness – growing in love and seeking after Christian perfection – could only be worked out with others. This is the basis of "social holiness." Wesley wrote in blunt terms about this conviction as early as 1739 in his 'Preface to Hymns and Sacred Poems': "Holy Solitaries" is a phrase no more consistent with the gospel than holy adulterers. The gospel of Christ knows of no religion, but social; no holiness but social holiness.

In passing, we must also be clear that for Wesley, pursuing social holiness is not directly equivalent to pursuing social justice. Social holiness is, distinctively, about finding, within Christian community, the necessary nourishment and feeding to grow. The fellowship of believers is the place where social holiness is cultivated and exercised and then crucially its impact is to move us out beyond any boundaries of the church and into the world.

So, Wesley's passion for the needs of the whole person led him to recognise that there is no holiness that is not social holiness. One of his descriptions of holiness was the renewal of the whole image of God and he affirmed that this was not to be understood in a purely individualistic way.

We see, then, that the dimensions of personal and social holiness are enmeshed and intertwined, relying one upon the other to enable all that God would wish to enable for us and through us.

Further affirmation of the significance of social holiness comes from Wesley's response, in 1749, to criticism that Methodist societies were divisive and were disrupting Christian fellowship in the established parishes. Wesley wrote: "But the fellowship you speak of never existed. Therefore it cannot be destroyed. Which of those true Christians ever had any such fellowship with these? Who watched over them in love? Who marked their growth in grace? Who advised and exhorted them from time to time? Who prayed with them and for them as they had need? This, and this alone is Christian fellowship. But alas! Where is it to be found? ...The real truth is just the reverse of this: we introduce Christian fellowship where it was utterly destroyed. And the fruits of it have been peace, joy, love and zeal for every good word and work."[41]

So, recognising holiness as essentially being seen through love of God and neighbour, Wesley constantly affirmed that holiness was a reality which needed to be lived out in community. This is why the building blocks of Methodism, the bands and classes, were so deeply significant. They provided the space for the messiness and pain of everyday life to be worked through within a context of growing in grace and love. Early Methodists were formed in the mind of Christ and learned together to walk as he walked.

As Teal puts it: "In early Methodism, social holiness began in small groups who helped one another grow in grace and love for God and neighbour."[42] Meadows adds: "This love was then to shine within a Methodist society by doing good to others in the community of faith, especially the poor. In short, social holiness refers to the love of God rooted in the heart of every believer and overflowing in ever-widening circles; from small groups, through the community of faith and out into the world."[43]

Scriptural Holiness through the Land

So, the pursuit of personal and social holiness – in itself a fulfilment of our mandate – provides the basis and indeed the impetus for "the people called Methodists" to then be active in spreading scriptural holiness through the land.

For Wesley this endeavour manifested itself in both the spiritual transformation of people's lives as they responded to the glorious Good News of Jesus and also the social transformation of the economic and political order of his time. This involved famously – and among many other things – fighting for the abolition of slavery and justice for the poor.

Our "divinely appointed mission", then, is nothing less than to look for God's gracious work in our own lives: being tuned by our fellowship and then, inevitably and purposefully, spilling out and provoking the transformation of the nation: in homes, schools, workplaces, universities, communities, national politics and so on. There is nowhere in the parish of the world where we are not called to be salt and light. We are called to be change-makers in the culture.

As Heath succinctly puts it: "The Wesleyan message offers a holistic gospel that heals and redeems body, mind, spirit, relationships, institutions and systems through the power of the Holy Spirit."[44]

For "the people called Methodists" grace is nothing less than the defining, shaping and underpinning energy that flows at the very heart of the movement.

Chapter 5

Captivated by Grace

In his book, 'What's So Amazing About Grace,' Philip Yancey tells of an encounter between C.S. Lewis and other scholars at a religious conference: "During a British conference on comparative religions, experts from around the world debated what, if any, belief was unique to the Christian faith. They began eliminating possibilities. Incarnation? Other religions had different versions of gods appearing in human form. Resurrection? Again, other religions had accounts of return from death. The debate went on for some time until C.S. Lewis wandered into the room. 'What's the rumpus about?' he asked and heard in reply that his colleagues were discussing Christianity's unique contribution among world religions. Lewis responded, 'Oh, that's easy — it's grace.'"[45]

God's boundless grace should indeed be regarded as a unique treasure of Christianity. However, historically "the people called Methodists" have lived out a particularly rich and distinctive appreciation of the transforming potential of grace to offer to the wider Christian family.

After many years of devoted service and a persevering determination to find a closer relationship with God, John Wesley came to powerfully recognise that God's outpouring of grace was absolutely key. He came to see that his deep-seated commitment to holiness could only truly be embraced through God's grace. Wesley came to describe grace as God's bounty or favour: "His free, undeserved favour ... man (sic) having no claim to the least of His mercies. It was free grace that formed man of the dust of the ground, and breathed into him a living soul and stamped on that soul the image of God, and put all things under His feet. ... for there is nothing we are or have or do, which can deserve the least thing at God's hand."[46]

So, for "the people called Methodists" grace is nothing less than the defining, shaping and underpinning energy that flows at the very heart of the movement. Grace is the fuel that energises the growth of God's people in holiness.

At a time when the church is prone to be almost paralysingly anxious that it is running low on resources of money, energy and even time, it surely should be of enormous reassurance to remember and affirm that the resource we most need – grace – is inexhaustible and in constant supply! So it is, that God's unconditional outpouring of unceasing grace is thoroughly, unadulterated, unending Good News.

How vitally important it is, therefore, that a continuing passionate appreciation and welcome of the unmerited provision of God's grace should continue to shape the life of "the people called Methodists."

As Methodism's "why" is rooted in being a movement committed to "spreading scriptural holiness,"[47] so the "how" is through consistently responding to, and then living responsibly in, God's grace.

The American United Methodist Book of Discipline helpfully defines grace as: "The undeserved, unmerited, and loving action of God in human existence through the ever-present Holy Spirit ... Grace pervades all of creation and is universally present. Grace is not a gift that God packages and bestows on us and creation. Grace is God's presence to create, heal, forgive, reconcile and transform human hearts, communities and the entire creation. Wherever God is present, there is grace! Grace brought creation into existence. Grace birthed human beings, bestowed on us the divine image, redeemed us in Jesus Christ and is ever transforming the whole creation into the realm of God's reign of compassion, justice, generosity and peace."[48]

Beck vividly scopes out the enormous significance of grace when he puts it like this: "Methodists continue to emphasise a personal experience of a seeking and sending trinitarian God, whose primary characteristic is relentless love. We experience the missional love of God through 'waves of grace' (prevenient, justifying and sanctifying) and 'means of grace' (prayer, searching scripture, communion, fasting and holy conversation). The discipleship process is connected to these means of grace and waves of grace, the profuse outflow of God's unconditional love."[49]

In his sermon, "The Scripture Way of Salvation"[50] Wesley summarises his understanding of the work of grace in saving and transforming human existence. He describes three movements of grace ("waves of grace" as Beck refers to them), and it is important to remind ourselves of them briefly.

Prevenient Grace: Grace that Goes Before

Prevenient grace is how Wesley described the bridging between God and humanity. Prevenient grace, writes Methodist scholar Charles Yrigoyen: "literally means the grace that 'comes before.' It is the grace of God that is 'free in all and free for all' and makes possible for everyone further response to God's forgiving and reconciling grace."[51]

We affirm, then, that prevenient grace is present in all creation – within human conscience, in the relationships and culture into which we are born. Love of family, activity within the Christian community, the sacraments, creation itself, pangs of conscience, the pull toward a vision of what can be – all these can be expressions of God's prevenient grace.

Wesley drew on St Augustine's writing about "preventing grace" to proclaim, as Beck puts it, that "preceding conscious awareness, God is after us, relentlessly pursuing us, protecting us. Realising that great love then moves us to accept our brokenness and engage God's transforming grace."[52] It is also deeply rooted within scripture, as we see God:

- wooing us as couples woo one another in a romantic relationship (Revelation 22:17),

- drawing us into a relationship (John 6:44-47),

- pursuing us so that the relationship is sustained (Romans 5:8),

- freeing us and enabling us to respond to God's offer of relationship (Romans 8:31-39) and

- empowering us to live in that relationship (Romans 5:6).

As Wesley said about his own recognition of prevenient grace: "If I were to write my own life, I should begin it before I was born."[53]

So, at the heart of our inheritance as "the people called Methodists" lies the belief that: "God's grace is available to all people and that it is active in people's lives long before they become aware of it. Wesleyan theology proposes that it is God's grace that restores in us the ability to respond in faith and that God's grace is what enables us to grow in faith throughout our lives. We also believe that it is God's grace that gives us assurance of our salvation. Because of the emphasis on the life of faith being pervaded by grace that comes, not from us, but from God, Methodists are inclined to be accepting and open, bearing in mind the potential of God's grace to work in everyone in varying ways."[54]

Wesley described prevenient grace as the porch of a house. It is where we prepare to enter the house. The process of receiving God's grace can also be compared to a journey. The desire to embark on the trip, the road or trail, the vehicle in which the journey is to be made and the map to be followed are all givens or gifts. The beauty of the landscape, the mind and eyes that imagined the journey and recognise its beauty, even the explorer who forged the trail are all unmerited gifts – grace!

But there is more to a house than the porch. There is more to a journey than the desire to travel. We must enter the house or begin the journey.

Justifying Grace: Grace that Puts Us Right

Prevenient grace prepares us to receive justifying grace. "Justification," said Wesley, "is another word for pardon. It is the forgiveness of all our sins, and ... our acceptance with God."[55]

Justifying grace then is the assurance of forgiveness that comes from accepting and receiving God's gracious gift of new life. It is being reconciled and realigned with God and discovering the richness of becoming part of the body of Christ.

Continuing the analogy of the house, Wesley considered justifying grace to be the doorway and the process of walking through it. The door is open with a welcome sign on it. God brings us reconciliation, adopts us into the life, death and resurrection of Jesus Christ, gives us our new identity as beloved sons and daughters and incorporates us into the body of Christ, the church.

Wesley's description of his experience at Aldersgate Street on 24 May 1738 perhaps portrays something rich of the meaning of justifying grace: "About a quarter before nine, while he [the leader] was describing the change which God works in the heart through faith in Christ, I felt my heart strangely warmed. I felt I did trust in Christ, Christ alone for salvation and an assurance was given me that He had taken away my sins, even mine, and saved me from the law of sin and death."[56]

Recognising ourselves as being rooted in the One who created us and breathed life into us is the essence of justifying grace. To accept that identity is to enter the doorway into a whole new existence. It is an identity we can never earn, nor one that can be taken from us.

Sanctifying Grace: Grace that Perfects

Wesley's understanding of grace then moves beyond our forgiveness and acceptance as precious children of God. God's goal is nothing less than the complete restoration of humankind into the image of God and the conforming of all creation to the image of Christ. Sanctification (from *sanctus* meaning 'holy') describes the ongoing process by which disciples are made holy and whole.

If prevenient grace is the porch of the house of grace and justifying grace is the doorway, sanctifying grace represents the rooms in the expansive dwelling of God's presence.

Sanctifying grace is God's freely given presence and power to restore us to the fullness of God's image in which we are created. Wesley talked, not without controversy, about sanctification in terms of Christian perfection by which he meant entire "holiness of heart and life." In his sermon 'Christian Perfection,' Wesley says that the possibility of Christian perfection does not imply Christians are exempt from ignorance, making mistakes, infirmities or being tempted. He offered perfection as another term for holiness. Sanctification, then, is the continuing process of being made perfect in love and of removing the desire to sin.

Growing through the Means of Grace

It seems to me to be so important for us to recover our appreciation that it is this constant flow of God's amazing grace that is the motivating and enabling energy of "the people called Methodists." Continuing to consistently be open to the waves of grace is the way in which we grow in holiness.

However, and crucially, as God's grace continues to flow into our lives, we all have our part to play in response. Wesley recognised that we need to develop patterns that can help us live responsibly with that grace.

This was a lesson he learned quickly as the early Methodist movement took shape, and it was because he did, that it was able to begin to fulfil its extraordinary mandate: of spreading scriptural holiness (and at the same time renewing the church). As people responded to Wesley's field preaching, he quickly came to observe that without appropriate follow up, the work was in vain. As he so bluntly put it: "I was more convinced than ever, that the preaching like an Apostle, without joining together those that are awakened, and training them up in the ways of God, is only begetting children for the murderer. How much preaching has there been for these twenty years all over Pembrokeshire! But no regular societies, no discipline, no order or connection; and the consequence is, that nine in ten of the once-awakened are now faster asleep than ever."[57]

So, a key part of Wesley's organising genius was to create "spaces for grace": the field, the society gathering, the class, the band; all places where people could receive and respond to the prevenient, justifying and sanctifying waves of grace. In these spaces mutual support and accountability blossomed and, decisively, the encouragement to all to practise the means of grace.

As Heath and Kisker put it: "These small groups [bands and classes] were so important to the revival that John [Wesley] committed never to preach where he could not immediately enfold someone who responded into a class ...The classes and bands were the instruments through which God worked to turn sinners into saints and by which a communal witness to God's intention for humanity (God's will and kingdom) was manifested."[58]

These "spaces for grace" are where we respond to the extraordinary waves of God's prevenient, justifying and sanctifying grace and where we are active and conscientious in our response – we live in what American Wesleyan, Randy Maddox calls "responsible grace."[59]

We see here, so clearly, the overlap between the last chapter's focus on growing in holiness and this chapter's focus on growing in grace. To recap, as we pursue our "why" of spreading scriptural holiness, we recognise that we need to grow in personal holiness and that this can only happen by taking our pursuit of social holiness seriously. Now we recognise that all of this journey depends on our continuing response to the flow of God's grace in our lives.

We grow in holiness as we continue to practise the means of grace: opening our lives obediently and deliberately to God's presence and power at work in us and the world. Growing in grace cannot be done within our own strength, but it does require us to be active and responsive. Maddox, very helpfully, describes this need for responsible grace as: "an abiding concern to preserve the vital tension between two truths that [Wesley] viewed as co-definitive of Christianity: without God's grace, we *cannot* be saved; while without our (grace-empowered but uncoerced) participation, God's grace *will not* save."[60]

This is so important for us as "the people called Methodists" to grasp: practising the means of grace lies at the heart of how we are able to fulfil our why and be the movement God called us to be. They are spiritual practices that enable us to receive and respond to God's grace. They are channels through which God's grace continues to flow into and through us.

Wesley described the means of grace, in his sermon of that title, as being: "outward signs, words, or actions, ordained of God, and appointed for this end, to be the ordinary channels whereby he might convey to men (sic), preventing, justifying, or sanctifying grace." Wesley's core "spaces for grace" (field, society, class and band gatherings) meant that people could, in different ways "watch over one another in love."

He identified several means of grace as primary:

- Worship and prayer: regular coming before God and communicating with God, including both personal and corporate prayer.

- Scripture reading: regular study and meditation on the Bible, both individually and in community.

- The sacraments: observing of baptism and Holy Communion as outward signs of God's grace.

- Fasting: an intentional practice of self-denial for spiritual purposes.

- Christian conferencing: engaging in intentional Christian community for the purpose of mutual accountability, encouragement and growth.

Additionally, Wesley pointed to acts of mercy and compassion as foundationally important. All of these are gifts by which we grow closer to Christ. All of these means of grace are not simply spiritual exercises for our own benefit but are the ways in which we open ourselves up to God's transforming grace in our lives. Through being "responsible", we continue to receive grace and grow in holiness.

Creating Spaces for Grace

I hope this chapter has persuasively made the case for recognising that receiving, and responding to, God's grace is absolutely essential for "the people called Methodists" to be able to fulfil our why of spreading scriptural holiness through the land.

An essential insight of Wesley was to recognise how his movement could continue to be fuelled by the ongoing waves of grace. As Beck puts it: "the true genius of the early Methodist movement was not only reaching people

In the 'fields' but inviting them into an intentional discipleship process that helped them along the journey of grace."[61]

It is good to note the recent emphasis within the Methodist Church around cultivating a Methodist Way of Life. As that continues to mature, it seems to me to be vitally important within that framework to purposefully affirm the significance of enabling "spaces for grace" and also our need to continue to grow in grace through embracing responsibly the means of grace.

Yancey, as he looked into the twenty-first century, observed: "I'm convinced that the future of the church in this new century depends on how well we master this notion of grace."[62] Rediscovering our appreciation, confidence and reliance on God's grace is surely absolutely core to us being rejuvenated as a movement of spiritual and social transformation.

REVIVE US AGAIN

*Here is the possibility, therefore,
of "the people called Methodists"
wonderfully honouring and
drawing on all our history
both as a movement
and as a church.*

Chapter 6

A "Both/And" People

It could be argued that Methodism has lived with something of an identity crisis for most of its life. Perhaps, to an extent at least, it has actually been there right from the start, within and emerging out of the very life and ministry of John Wesley.

Wesley, as Anglican Priest, remained thoroughly committed to seeing the Methodist movement as a renewing force within the Church of England (and beyond) rather than a separate church.[63] Indeed, flourishing as a movement within the Church of England was one of the ways in which Wesley hoped to influence and renew the wider church, as we will explore more fully later.

However, as the movement grew, it became increasingly difficult for it to be held within the Church of England. Step by step, the shape of the movement gradually became, through its ministry and organisation, ever more like that of an ordered, separated Church.

The fault-lines between Methodist societies and church, movement and institution, organism and organisation have arguably endured ever since. These fault-lines are, therefore, in a sense, part of the inherited cultural definition of who we are. They are just *there* – part of the air we breathe and the water in which we swim.

This is not just a matter of historic or academic debate, primarily about our past. These tensions and uncertainties about who we are raise their heads, whether acknowledged as such or not, again and again in exploring our sense of calling, and how we should view our mission and ministry. They are there in the midst of, for example, our ecumenical conversations, our view of ordination and our wonderings about the future.

At their most unhelpful, the fault-lines present as tensions which almost paralyse: holding us in a state of limbo. On the one hand, dynamic and energetic impulses as a movement are too often stifled; on the other hand, heightened anxieties emerge about long-term sustainability and credibility as a "fully-fledged" church.

So, Who are We?

It is important to be as clear about "who" we are as "why" we are. Purpose and identity are both key to shaping culture, or as is often described, "the way we do things around here." Rejuvenating a clear sense of Methodism's identity has the potential to guide the journey ahead far more powerfully than all the reports and statements that may be produced, worthy and helpful as they so often are. Much more than any concerns about the future survival and health of the Methodist Church, this matters for the sake of the world, and for the sharing of the Gospel within that world in the twenty-first century.

I recognise a growing sense of urgency about clarifying identity, evidenced by various factors aligning to make this time feel like a God-given "kairos" moment:

- The inexorable and continuing decline in numbers, breadth and depth of the current Methodist Church in Britain (as previously explored) which, when honestly faced, force the questioning of the medium-term sustainability of inherited models.

- The developing life and growth of the Fresh Expressions movement. Methodism was a founding partner in this movement and continues to play a significant role. The recently adopted Evangelism and Growth Strategy deepens Methodism's commitment to creating "Church at the Margins" and "New Places for New People."[64] This needs a careful working out of how the resulting diversity of expressions of ministry and mission are appropriately valued, encouraged and enabled to have the space they need to flourish, alongside inherited models of church and received understandings of ecclesial identity.

- The ongoing ecumenical conversations, particularly with covenanted partner, the Church of England, holding with them the enduring hopes that a greater sense of meaningful unity can be achieved.

So, it seems to be most definitely time for a renewed understanding of the purpose and identity of "the people called Methodists!"

Celebrating "Both/And"

I want to make a case that what is NOT needed here is a polarised, binary choice: essentially around opting either to be a movement or a church. We don't need to choose between two alternative ways of seeing ourselves – one "correct" and one "wrong" — quite the opposite!

Instead, I see huge potential in imaginatively and openly embracing an identity as *both* a movement *and* a church. This could be an enormous gift both to ourselves and to the wider church. I believe it can both help breathe life into the inherited church and provide a helpful rootedness to fresh expressions of church.

"The people called Methodists" began as a movement within a church, and then became a church that retained a sense of movement. Can a way now be crafted, with a truly liberating sense of ease, that imaginatively and confidently blends both these riches?

I believe that this proposition is far from being a cop-out; simply dodging the hard choice of one over the other. Neither can I begin to imagine that God wants us to be stymied by an anxiety-filled introspection about our continuing existence, especially given the unwavering urgency of our divinely appointed mission.

Significantly, I believe that this vision of truly celebrating our identity as a "movement/ church" offers us a recovery of a "both/and" approach that lay at the heart of Wesley's pragmatic developing of the early movement. This "both/ and" understanding actually contains the potential to take a hold of something that has, in our best moments, been both instinctive and distinctive.

The prominence of "conjunctive" (both/and) theology as core to Wesley and our history has been explored by many Methodist theologians and historians. American Pastor, Drew McIntyre, helpfully reflects on its distinctive positives: "I recall vividly when Randy Maddox, in one of my classes on the history and theology of Methodism, said that Wesley 'held things together that other Christians pushed apart'. I am still floored by the degree to which this statement is true. Wesley loved the Church Fathers and contemporary theologians of his day. He was a loyal Anglican even though his efforts were often unsupported. He appreciated the Book of Common Prayer and extemporaneous prayer. He loved Scripture but also recognised the need for community in spiritual formation ... Wesley also loved the sacraments but wasn't above preaching in a field or on top of a grave to reach the people he needed to reach. In other words, Methodists at our core are 'both-and' rather than 'either-or' Christians. We are naive enough to believe that we really should have our cake and eat it ... He brought things together from many different traditions in a unique and interesting synthesis."[65]

Beck, writing from his Methodist and Fresh Expressions background in the United States, recognises the potential of such a positive conjunctive theology as he explores his sense of call to take the "seeds of Wesley's organising principles and practices, then replant them on the new missional frontier ... for instance, the greatest 'and' of the Methodist movement is rarely even recognised. John Wesley was a faithful Anglican priest until the day he died and a missional renegade who preached in the fields. He sustained a tether back to the inherited church and encouraged people to participate fully in her life, and yet where church structures constrained the focus on missional evangelism, he 'laid them aside.' He was a man who challenged the inherited system deeply, while trying to bring renewal to it. He held together competing ideas that divided believers in his day in creative tension."[66]

Methodist minister and scholar, David Lowes Watson expresses similar thinking when he explores the model of "ecclesiolae in ecclesia" (little churches in the big church). He recognises that the "spiritual freedom of the little church prevents discipleship from becoming unduly regulated or legalistic; the doctrine and structure of the larger church guard against spiritual licence and excess. When equal emphasis is given to spirit and structure, the ministry and mission of the church are powerful and healthy."[67] Although originally that sense of being "ecclesiolae in ecclesia" was to be within the Church of England it has, in part at least, developed into our cultural understanding of connexionalism.

What Watson describes here inspires me to press the case for a renewed, relaxed, expansive and permissive-giving culture and self-understanding of who we are as a "movement/church." This recognition as sharing together in being a "both/and" people can be a great gift:

- to ourselves (we relax!),

- to the inherited church (we can be authentic and effective, to our calling to renew the church) and

- to the Fresh Expressions movement as it seeks ways to embody the new alongside the historic (we can provide a rootedness which is resourcing and protecting without being smothering or constraining).

Here is the possibility, therefore, of "the people called Methodists" wonderfully honouring and drawing on all our history both as a movement and as a church. How wonderful it would be to integrate the riches of both in a way which renews the inherited and empowers the emerging.

As I say, I most definitely do not see this as a cop-out – it is not easy! Nonetheless, it offers us the chance to recalibrate our view of some things, relax about others and, crucially, re-prioritise around the mobilising why. Methodism cannot be everything, nor has God ever asked it to be! But if we can cultivate a relaxed ecclesiology that doesn't over-stress about whether our ecumenical credentials will "pass muster" in all quarters, we may well find that ecumenical contributions will actually be more effective.

Theologian and author, Martyn Percy, writing in 'Unmasking Methodist Theology,' pressed the case for Methodism to re-discover its movement-roots. (It should be noted that this was written in 2004, and some may want to take issue with his assumptions about the future of Wales!). Also, although I am enthusiastically arguing the case for not opting for one understanding over another, his thoughts still have merit as they articulate, I think, something important about how Methodism's self-understanding can be renewed:

"It is my belief that Methodism should focus and reflect on its core strength – those gifts and charisms that gave it a strong movement identity in the first place. It has a clear future as a movement. It is also apparent that an explicit ecclesiology can be developed from its core strength. But this does not necessarily mean that it need continue to be an independent denomination, or indeed even act as a 'church' per se. Perhaps Methodism is rather like Wales. It is a distinctive principality rather than a full-blown country: its future is only secure in a United Kingdom. To follow this analogy through, I see no reason why Methodism cannot function like Quakerism, with people either belonging exclusively to such movements, or belonging to a church or denomination and the movement: carrying, in effect, dual passports. In other words, we are back to the future. It should be possible to be an Anglican, and to be a Methodist, with Methodism no longer describing a denominational label, but rather a particular spirituality and form of methodical discipleship. Methodism, then, as an intelligible and vibrant movement, is more like the leaven in the lump than even it may ever have realised. I suspect that the future of Methodism – at least in Britain – may lie in the Church saving itself from becoming too 'churchy': a poor cousin of modernity. Habitually, all churches recover something of their colour when they cease to be comfortable and begin to look urgent. So instead of trying to operate like a modernist meta-organisation, Methodism may need to revisit some of its primary and generative spiritual roots. To return to being a movement and, in so doing, to renew not only itself but also those other denominations around it that undoubtedly need to learn from the fusion of its dynamic evangelistic heritage and capacious social witness. To be sure, this would be a costly decision. To journey from being a movement to a church, and then back to being a movement, is not a development that many in the Conference ... would welcome. But I wonder what the Wesley brothers would have had to say about it?"[68]

"Both/And" – a "Blended Ecology"

What I am encouraging here can be expressed as a "blended ecology." It was the former Archbishop of Canterbury, Rowan Williams, who coined the phrase "mixed economy." Others in the UK have developed instead the phrase "mixed ecology," drawing on the rich and powerful agricultural imagery of field, seed and harvest. In the United States, some – including Beck – talk of "blended ecology." I warm to this phrase and the vision of developing a life as circuits and connexion as a blended ecology that:

- allows all sorts of expressions of mission, community and witness to be mutually supportive, equally valued and encouraged,

- blends with a consistency of love, respect, honouring and appreciation of all that is inherited and what is new and emerging and

- enables the old to be renewed by the new and the new to be informed by the old.

It is helpful to observe that, even in the development of the early church as described in the Acts of the Apostles, we see both the emergence of structure and practice alongside the persistent and ongoing move of God's Spirit in prompting new missionary adventures onwards and outwards: from centre to the edge, but always with a commitment to holding everything together. Tensions inevitably arise and things need working out, for example, in the Council of Jerusalem in Acts 15. However, such is the recognition of the mandate of God's people that the tensions are overcome, and the movement continues to grow, whilst embraced within the emerging solidity of church networks. Beck describes the relationships as "deep roots, wild branches." Both were important.

What a precious gift, then, that 'the people called Methodists" can receive and then offer to the wider church in this twenty-first century: the opportunity to embrace with confidence a "blended ecology," that celebrates the authenticity of our "both/and" Wesley-an approach, delighting in being a "movement/church" – all for the sake of the world with whom God continues to invite us to share the wonderful Gospel of Jesus Christ.

REVIVE US AGAIN

So, here is the dream of our connexionalism being a dynamic custodian and enduring reminder of our compelling why.

Chapter 7

Celebrating Unity in Our Diversity

Martyn Atkins, missiologist and former General Secretary of the Methodist Church in Britain, highlights the unusual (to our modern day) spelling of "connexion" when he humorously refers to it as the "X factor of Methodism."[69] He is emphasising something significant about how a movement of spiritual and social transformation can be sustained and empowered: through the potential for every diverse strand to be creatively and powerfully connected.

More than that, and to emphasise some earlier themes, we need to see how "connexion" is part and parcel of a Methodist way of understanding our personal Christian life. As we have already recognised, we are never to be solo Methodists! "For Methodists, connexionalism is not an abstract principle or a piece of historical baggage, but a way of being Christian."[70]

Sweet talks of it like this: "*With* is the contact word, the embrace of grace. We are passionate about the contacts and connections that constitute a person. A person is never a solo individual. A person is always a web of 'withs', a network of relationships with ramifications that ripple out into the world. Methodism's trinitarian concept of God is by definition relational. The primacy of relations in both the divine and the human is the prized heirloom of our family silver."[71]

Recognising the centrality of connection as part and parcel of a thriving church, 'Called to Love and Praise' puts it like this: "From its beginnings, Methodism has been pragmatic in its approach to questions of church structure and order. Its own order and discipline emerged largely as the result of a series of *ad hoc* experiments. They were created in the 'missionary' situation of the eighteenth century, and the legacy of this has been a tendency to subordinate church order to, and to deploy church resources in response to, the missionary needs of the Church. This is, or should be, a particular strength of a 'connexional' Church, in which there is a common recognition that all are parts of a larger whole."[72]

In 2017, the Methodist Church reaffirmed the significance of connexion through a report, 'The Gift of Connexionalism in the Twenty-first Century.' That report affirmed: "All Christians are essentially linked to one another; no Local Church is or can be an autonomous unit complete in itself. This understanding of the essence of the Church is grounded in the New Testament. It is vital for effective mission and it is expressed in apt structures of oversight, balancing authority and subsidiarity. Where these insights have become part of the ethos of the Church, connexionalism is experienced in a way of life which assumes that all contribute to and receive from the life and mission of the whole Church."[73]

However, I am reasonably certain that seasoned Methodists will recognise that very often the word "connexion" is misappropriated to imply an understanding of referring to "head office" or the "centre" rather than describing a "being in relationship" (with) which is every bit as much, if not more, about the "circumference." All too often it is also used in ways which imply it is mainly about "authority" or "power" or "rules." How urgent, therefore, is the need to rediscover its galvanising potential as really being all about relationships, about a way of understanding ourselves as people together and about enabling us to better fulfil our divinely appointed mission?

Let's Start From the Other Way Round!

So, let me explore the essence of "connexion" by turning the commonly held views the other way around.[74] Let us view "being in connexion" from the circumference, the grass roots and from any and every part of the land (and also keeping very much in mind those not yet touched by the reach of a renewed movement of spiritual and social transformation).

How is it that being in connexion can play a vital part in supporting and sustaining the life and mission of everyone who is part of "the people called Methodists?"

Firstly, let us remember that we are all embraced together in God's mission. This means that we should be reinforcing for ourselves and each other a self-understanding of being part of God's mission with a church, rather than a church with a mission. So, any and every sense of connexion is about serving God's mission, and never an end in itself.

With a focus that is rooted in God's transformative mission to every tribe and tongue ("through the land") we can see that a genuine understanding of connexion should be about connecting, energising and releasing a huge and extraordinary diversity of experience, culture, context and expression of faith. This presents an immediate and necessary challenge to what can so easily become default thinking or natural operating mode: that institutional and organisational tendency which can lead us to plump for an understanding and/or practice of connexionalism which works towards uniformity.

I therefore want to reclaim what I see to be an authentically Wesley-an view of connexionalism as embracing the exact opposite. It presents what perhaps sounds initially like a more demanding path to tread but I believe it is the more faithful – and much more life-giving way – of seeking to pursue our divinely appointed why: seeing connexion as a celebration and encouragement of our diversity. Treasuring our being in connexion as an adventure of recognising how to share in a glorious unity whilst simultaneously and intentionally developing extraordinary variety and diversity in mission and ministry.

As God in Jesus moved into a specific, physical local neighbourhood, rooted in time, context and culture, so we are called to be the body of Christ expressing the Good News of the Kingdom in every context and culture. Christ's incarnation was to a particular place and context but so that ultimately God's saving love might be shared universally. As I have previously affirmed, to "spread scriptural holiness through the land" must mean including to every corner, every tribe, every context, every part of the land.

Whilst human civilisation has always contained huge diversity, that diversity within our own land is arguably greater today than ever – languages, backgrounds, sexualities, ethnicities, world views etc. Another feature of the twenty-first century is the transient flow patterns of people's lives: where we work, sleep, volunteer, practice our hobbies, together with, for many, an intuitive, instinctive and constant interrelationship with the digital world.

A Celebration of Diversity

Connexion is *not* about reaching into that diversity and bringing a homogenous blending. We really must not let connexionalism ever imply uniformity. It should be the opposite!

It is no triumph of connexionalism that one can go to so many churches in different parts of the land on a Sunday morning and still find what is taking place to be so very similar to what is happening in so many other gatherings. No! Connexionalism's gift surely is to be enabling and creating such an effective and missionally-minded network and tapestry that it is fanning the flames of spreading holiness across the land through ongoing openness to God's grace – every person and every "space for grace" playing their own distinctive part.

Picture for a moment a Crown™ 75 paint chart. Their website boasts hundreds of different shades and variants. They aim to provide a shade for every context. Whatever colours are present within the space to be painted can find their Crown match with a shade that has already been produced or by mixing what is already there to create something bespoke. But, of course, we don't then look at a wall carrying a particular colour and instantly recognise that as a Crown product! So, what makes Crown "Crown?" What is their distinctive? Why would the Crown company hope that people go to *their* paint chart or mixing station and choose their paint?

It is not about the shade. No — Crown hopes that people will choose their paint because they have earned customers' trust in the quality of the paint, whatever the shade. There is, they hope, something distinctive that means customers have confidence in choosing their paint and in discovering precisely the right shade for their context.

When I started pursuing this analogy I began by looking at another paint company but then was drawn to Crown through their mission statement: "It's not just paint, it's personal." This chimed richly with my thinking about connexion. (I also then noticed on their website the account of the company's history — stretching from 1777 to the present day — largely overlapping the history of "the people called Methodists"!)[76]

So, a significant part of Wesley's example was to travel to the fields, to become more vile, that he might reach out to as many different types of people as possible. The vision then is of a huge kaleidoscope of shades creating the connexion, not a blending into some "Methodist magnolia." The potential genius of the Methodist Connexion is about ensuring that within every shade context, the diverse and particular charisms of grace and life can grow; that in every shade of life our distinctive mission of enabling people to receive the Kingdom of God, and growing in social holiness, can lead to the spreading of scriptural holiness: the spiritual and social transformation of the world.

Although it may to some sound like this makes the Methodist Connexion more tenuous, I would maintain it offers the potential to make it far richer and effective.

The 2006 book, 'The Starfish and the Spider: The Unstoppable Power of Leaderless Organisations' shines some illustrative light on this.[77] It is an invigorating read exploring some fascinating organisational theory, from the perspective of the differences between a starfish and a spider. Although a starfish and a spider may superficially appear similar, they have a fundamentally different structure. If a spider's leg is cut off, it is crippled. If its head is cut off, it dies. But if a starfish's leg is cut off it grows a new one, and the old leg can grow into an entirely new starfish.   The spider and the starfish have very contrasting biological natures: the spider's head controls the body whereas starfish have a decentralised neural structure which permits regeneration.

The book goes on to look at models of both centralised and decentralised leadership, then exploring the potential of being a hybrid organisation, which seems to speak powerfully into the possibilities for a revitalising of connexion – a dynamic network, each and every bit playing its part and contributing to its purpose – spreading scriptural holiness through the land. Wow!

So, here is the dream of our connexionalism being:

- a dynamic custodian and enduring reminder of our compelling why,

- a way of describing the distinctive motivations for an ever-increasing palette of shades of mission and ministry,

- a reminder of the essential value in our interconnectedness as "the people called Methodists,"

- a fluid but energising network of encouragement and support: a vibrant web of relationships ensuring that Methodist charisms are fleshed out, enabled and brought to life in every context and culture.

Reclaiming the Missional Potential of Connexionalism

As the Methodist Connexion originally came to life, people, and quickly then societies, were connected to Wesley himself. This meant they were under his care, his watch, his oversight. That included discipline but, also crucially, the encouragement to stay close to each other, to take seriously the call to social holiness and to encourage each other to (a) do no harm, (b) do good and (c) stay in love with God.

Atkins emphases the potential here as he writes: "By describing ourselves as a Connexion of itself suggests that we understand our origins in terms of being a movement rather than, primarily, a church in classical terms. We were originally "a people called Methodists" because we were 'in connexion' with Mr Wesley, and so readily entered into the sharing of doctrines (and doctrinal emphases), 'discipline' and the deploying of resources for the common good. We have always stated our readiness to change our rules in obedience to God's leading about our calling and purposes. We have adapted in order to meet mission imperatives in the past and can and must do so again. At our best we do permit grace, not law, to guide us. Our present focus on discipleship and mission is a proper expression of our mutual connectedness today. After John Wesley's death Methodists became 'in connexion' with and through the Conference. This assumed an understanding of discipleship in which individuals accepted their part in contributing to the life of the Connexion within local societies and so making plain from the beginning that Christianity was no solitary or simply personal thing, but was lived out on a big map. "We" and "us", at least in terms of our rules and practices, took primacy over "me" and "I."[78]

As we look to fulfilling our sacred mandate, our why of spreading scriptural holiness through the land, a revitalised appreciation of connexionalism assumes urgent significance. As Beck puts it: "Denominations have tried top-down leadership strategies to reverse decline for decades; perhaps we need to give local, grassroots revolutionaries a chance. We need cohorts of local church leaders who will dig into their contexts and resist the urge to climb the corporate ladders of denominational success."[79]

A renewed relational appreciation of what it is to be "in connexion" is surely a gift of great value for "the people called Methodists" as we journey forward. As we celebrate our historic "divinely appointed mission" and also celebrate the developing fruitfulness of Fresh Expressions, it can surely inspire and resource our growth — enthusiastically embracing our identity as a creative and rich blended ecology of the inherited and the new.

Our history as both an apostolic, renewing movement and as a mature expression of church has rich potential to contribute rich gifts for the renewing of the wider church (inherited and new) for these days.

Chapter 8

Renewing the Church

We have already seen that a key part of Methodism's enduring "why", alongside "spreading scriptural holiness" is to "renew the church." This element of the Methodist mandate was deeply rooted within Wesley's heart and mind, fuelled by the frustrations that arose within him as he looked at much of the established church around him. He was passionately keen to develop what he called a "practical divinity" which might emulate that of the early church.

Given that early and foundational impetus and commitment, it is important to appreciate and reclaim, this significant element of what it is to be "the people called Methodists." For Wesley, this renewal of the church was about recovering the essence of practical divinity. British Methodist Minister, Rupert Davies in his book 'Methodism' summarised these "dominant characteristics" as seven points where early Methodism echoed the early Church:

1. A complete and whole-hearted acceptance of the cardinal doctrines of the Christian faith, as conveniently laid down in the historic creeds, combined with the conviction that doctrine which is not proved in devotion and life and does not issue in practical charity is valueless; in the last resort, "experimental religion" (as John Wesley called it) is greatly preferable to doctrinal orthodoxy, if the choice has to be made between them.

2. The insistence that the heart of Christianity lies in the personal commerce of a man (sic) with his Lord, who has saved him and won the forgiveness of his sins and will live in him to transform his character.

3. The stress on the doctrine of the Holy Spirit, the Person of the Trinity who is often neglected by institutional Christianity, yet without whom neither the fulfilment of the Lord's commandments nor the common life of the Christian community is more than a vague aspiration.

4. The earnest and patient attempt to embody the 'life in Christ' of which the New Testament speaks, in personal and social 'holiness' and the formation for this purpose of small groups of committed people who will encourage, correct, instruct, edify and support each other.

5. The desire to make known the Gospel, and above everything else the love and pity of God for each individual sinner, on the widest possible scale and in the most persuasive terms.

6. A generous concern for the material as well as the spiritual welfare of the underprivileged.

7. The development of a Church Order in which the laity stands alongside the ministry, with different but equally essential functions, sharing with the ministry in the tasks of preaching the Gospel, caring for the Christian flock and administering the Church's affairs.[80]

Writing in 'Forgotten Ways: Reactivating the Missional Church', Missiologist Alan Hirsch explores the dominant modes of the church in three eras.[81] He acknowledges that this is inevitably a simplification of the actual situation (as real life is not that easily categorised) and yet it offers a fascinating analysis, as we think about the early church and any attempt to take hold again of all that was good about it:

	APOSTOLIC AND POSTAPOSTOLIC MODE (AD32 to 313)	CHRISTENDOM MODE (313 to current)	EMERGING MISSIONAL MODE (past 40 years)
Locus of Gathering	Does not have dedicated sacral buildings; often underground and persecuted.	Buildings become central to the notion, and experience, of church.	Rejects the concern and need for dedicated "church" buildings. Incorporates second and third places.
Leadership Ethos	Leadership operating with at least a five-fold ministry-leadership ethos as in Ephesians 4 (apostle, prophet, evangelist, pastor, teacher).	Leadership by ordained clergy, thus creating a professional guild operating primarily in a shepherd-teacher mode.	Leadership embraces a pioneering-innovative mode including a five-fold ministry-leadership ethos. Ordination is not essential or even desired.
Organisational Structure(s)	Grassroots, decentralised, network, cellular, movemental.	Institutional forms, hierarchical (top-down) notion of leadership, centralised structures.	Move back to more grassroots, decentralised, movemental, hybrid.
Sacramental Mode (means of grace)	Communion celebrated as a community meal in houses; baptism by everyone.	Increasing institutionalisation of grace through the sacraments which can be experienced only "in church" and handled by priesthood.	Redeems, and innovates new symbols, rituals, and events; democratization of the sacraments; recovery of the meal/hospitality.
Position in Society	Church is on the margins of society, illegitimate and largely underground.	Church is perceived as central to society and surrounding culture, the only legitimate religion.	Church is once again on the fringes of society and culture, increasing marginalization, less legitimacy.
Missional-Mode	Missionary, incarnational, transforming, sending church.	Attractional, maintenance of religious order, defensive.	Missional; incarnational-sending; The church re-embraces a missional stance in relation to culture.

It seems to me that this analysis chimes strongly with Wesley's own view all those years before when he said: "Persecution never did, never could give any lasting wound to genuine Christianity. But the greatest it ever received, the grand blow which was struck at the very root of that humble, gentle, patient love, which is the fulfilling of the Christian law, the whole essence of true religion, was struck in the fourth century by Constantine the Great, when he called himself a Christian, and poured in a flood of riches, honours, and power upon the Christians, more especially upon the clergy."[82]

What is striking to observe in Hirsch's overview is that the early Methodist movement, in general terms, embodied much within the third column. The movement was developing a contextually appropriate re-working of the early church's missional beginnings. However, as time has passed, so the movement has become increasingly institutional, increasingly adopting patterns and practices found more identifiably within the middle column.

By contrast today, so very much further down a road of post-Christendom than was ever contemplated in Wesley's day, we see much of the third column within the burgeoning Fresh Expressions movement.[83] We could almost say that the early growing Methodist movement was a forerunner of so much that we now celebrate as Fresh Expressions.

However, again, I am wanting to be careful not to throw the baby away with the bath water! I want to see the providence and goodness of God in all that has gone before. "We know that all things work together for good for those who love God, who are called according to his purpose" declares the apostle Paul.[84] So, I repeat my conviction that it is time for "the people called Methodists" to truly become a blended ecology.

Does this not provide such an encouraging and hopeful platform for the Methodist Church in the twenty-first century? Ought this not to be the natural role and place for us? There is so much about our inherited structures and possibilities that remain as embedded coding within our Standing Orders and "ways of being" from our earliest days.

Revitalised and re-imagined, they could truly rejuvenate Methodism. Our history as both an apostolic, renewing movement and as a mature expression of church has rich potential to contribute rich gifts for the renewing of the wider church (inherited and new) for these days.

Hirsch and fellow missiologist Dave Ferguson observe that every historical renewal movement "recovers some degree of the following movemental elements: priesthood of believers, 'kingdom of God' over 'church', prophetic protest, church planting, or mission on the fringes and among the poor."[85] These elements describe so much of what early Methodism was and my dream is that we can recover that life and passion of being a dynamic renewal movement/church, responding to God's heart and mission.

In rediscovering momentum as a blended ecology some of that early Methodist fire can help fuel the fulfilling of the vision expressed in the "God for All" strategy of the Methodist Church's Evangelism and Growth team: "The Methodist Church is committed to being a growing, evangelistic, inclusive, justice-seeking Church – so that new people become disciples of Jesus Christ, faith deepens for everyone, and diverse communities and churches experience transformation."[86]

Although the brutal reality of the statistics of the last decades makes the Methodist Church increasingly aware of its decline, still the words of missiologist and theologian, David Bosch ring true when, in 'Transforming Mission,' he wrote: "Strictly speaking one ought to say that the church is always in a state of crisis and that its greatest shortcoming is that it is only occasionally aware of it ... This ought to be the case because of the abiding tension between the church's essential nature and its empirical condition ... That there were so many centuries of crisis-free existence for the church was therefore an abnormality... And if the atmosphere of 'crisislessness' still lingers on in many parts of the west, this is simply the result of a dangerous delusion. Let us also know that to encounter crisis is to encounter the possibility of truly being the church."[87]

Could it be then that the crisis of institutional decline (and some significant dying) could, most wonderfully, trigger the resurrection of "the people called Methodists" to be re-awakened as a movement/church which is both truly willing and empowered to renew the church?

So, at the heart of seeking to fulfil the mandate lies the need to recover a deep understanding that we are not a church with a mission, but a church responding to God's mission.

Chapter 9

Giving Ourselves Away with Godly Zeal

It's Not About "Us!"

I am all too well aware that there is a thorny irony to be grasped in a good deal of what I have so far set out: much attention has been given to the nature of "us" – and the developing of the idea of "us" — "the people called Methodists" — as a conduit of renewal, embracing a "both/and" blended ecology. Yes, my burden and passion here is of imagining the re-missioning of "the people called Methodists." However, it is important to affirm that any thoughts of a rescue or revitalisation plan for "us" as being an end in itself is a wholly flawed starting (or end!) point.

No, we must be clear that our attention, priority, focus and enduring passion need to be about seeking God's heart of love for the whole of creation and responding to that love and living life in tune with God's priorities. That lies at the very heart of our divinely appointed mission. Indeed, "one of the most important things Christians need to know about the church is that the church is not of ultimate importance."[88]

Yes, God has certainly chosen the church to be a key part of the mission but she is subsidiary to this key mind-blowing, life-changing, transformative truth: God is on a mission to draw the world close, to save and make whole, to welcome home, and all with the ultimate promise of a new heaven and a new earth.

Therefore, as Beck puts it, "God has a mission; thus, there is a church"[89] and God has commissioned the church to join in that mission. The church does not have any mission other than the pure privilege of joining in with the mission of God. Theologian Jurgan Moltmann puts it like this: "Mission does not come from the church; it is from mission and in light of mission that the church has to be understood."[90]

So, my focus on "us" is with the fervent hope that by allowing God's renewing Spirit to blow through our whole being afresh; we can be drawn more deeply into God's heart and thereby be liberated more fully to share God's heart.

This genuine and thorough self-giving is most fully exemplified in Jesus Christ. In this remarkable passage in Philippians 2:5-11, we see the self-emptying ("kenosis") of Christ: "Let the same mind be in you that was in Christ Jesus, who, though He was in the form of God, did not regard equality with God as something to be exploited, but emptied Himself, taking the form of a slave; being born in human likeness. And being found in human form, He humbled Himself and became obedient to the point of death – even death on a cross. Therefore God also highly exalted Him and gave Him the name that is above every name, so that at the name of Jesus every knee should bend, in heaven and on earth and under the earth, and every tongue should confess that Jesus Christ is Lord, to the glory of God the Father."

See how these verses set out the way Jesus models and embodies for us the self-emptying of Himself, so that He could fully enter into the realities of the world within, in His earthly life, a particular context and culture?

Here is something for us to emulate all over again, in a way that Wesley also exemplified as he set aside his own preferences for the sake of the gospel. My sincere hope is that we can find freedom from our understandable but ultimately fruitless introspection; freedom from anxieties about our institutional survival and freedom from what sometimes feels like an endless preference for deciding it is "time to talk about the church", rather than "time to talk about God."

It should be of little surprise, of course, that we have gradually and unintentionally tended towards becoming self-absorbed and introspective. It is entirely natural within the usual life cycle of institutions. As our history, being and story have grown, so, inevitably, has a centre of gravity, a stability, a past to be honoured and borne in mind and a sense, sometimes, that our heritage is a primary dimension to be protected. But as management consultant Peter Drucker plainly and forcibly puts it: "People in any organisation are always attached to the obsolete – the things that should have worked but did not, the things that once were productive and no longer are."[91]

American Christian author and sociologist, Tony Campolo tells the story of a large oil refinery, using all the best techniques of chemical engineering. It was an impressive structure and every effort was made to ensure that everything was in perfect working order. One day, some visitors toured the plant. They were shown, with due pride, all the various chambers and pipework and machinery. Near the end of the tour, one of the visitors asked if they could see the shipping department. 'What do you mean?' asked the guide. 'Well, where you ship out all the gasoline and oil you process here,' said the visitor. 'Ah, we don't have any shipping department,' answered the guide. 'You see, all the energy products produced in this refinery are used for keeping the refinery going.'[92]

There is dangerous truth in the story. Maintaining "church" can take up so much energy and resource in "keeping the show on the road" that we lose sight of God's captivating mission in which we should be both found and held and also commissioned and sent out.

So, at the heart of seeking to fulfil the mandate lies the need to recover a deep understanding that we are not a church with a mission, but a church responding to God's mission.

As Wesleyan scholar and author, Howard Snyder puts it: "The church gets into trouble whenever it thinks it is in the church business rather than the Kingdom business. In the church business, people are concerned with church activities, religious behaviour and spiritual things. In the Kingdom business, people are concerned with Kingdom activities, all human behaviour and everything God has made. Church people think about how to get people into the church; Kingdom people think about how to get the church into the world."[93]

If we dare to believe that we can re-discover a renewing of the distinctive mission and practice, then it needs to be within this light and truth. As Beck highlights, as the church flows from the mission of God, so mission should birth structures. "As mission takes shape so does the church. Structures should enable mission."[94]

And All with Godly Zeal!

"Unfaltering resolve." I feel more than slightly embarrassed to have to admit, with my lifetime in Methodism, that it was only recently that I really took notice of this phrase in the Deed of Union and was then struck so forcibly by it. There this phrase lies, at the heart of our mandate – our why. Our mutual commitment: with "unfaltering resolve!"

It powerfully resonates with the way in which the early "people called Methodists" lived. They were frequently derided for their expressions of faithful living that were passionate and full of zeal. That zeal came from their rooted-in-God confidence. Although there seems to be no evidence that John Wesley actually said: "Catch on fire with enthusiasm and people will come for miles to watch you burn" (though it is frequently attributed to him), the phrase nonetheless bears testimony to his impact on individuals, communities and, ultimately, the nation. Those early Methodists demonstrated what an extraordinary impact an assured and passionate love for God and fellow humanity can have.

It is worth remembering that, in the early days, the term "the people called Methodists" was used as a term of denigration. The very word "Methodist" was a way of ridiculing the habits of the Oxford Holy Club that Wesley was a part of, with its earnest and rigorous discipline in pursuing a life of holiness and seeking to be the best disciples of Christ they could be.

Wesley's journey into being filled with Godly zeal was quite a journey. Formative moments were that Holy Club and later his fateful and fear-filled journey to, and time in, Georgia. This led to many struggles before the heart-warming assurance of the Aldersgate experience of 1738. This Godly zeal to see spiritual and social transformation mobilised Wesley to do that which he considered more vile – moving out of the church to the fields, to where the people were. As Beck puts it "a heart set on fire with the love of God can't contain the flames."[95]

There were further struggles to come, as his journal makes crystal clear. But the Godly zeal also gave Wesley the persistence and inspiration to weave together "a robust system that combined discipleship with ethics, while creating a relational network that would sustain the movement beyond his own influence."[96]

As Wesley's zeal for holiness grew through his ever-deepening appreciation of God's grace, Methodists came to be also disdainfully called "enthusiasts" and "reasonable enthusiasts." The reasonable enthusiasts tag came from another "both/and" Wesley-an attribute of cultivating a passionate spirituality that balanced reason and experience. The word enthusiasm is derived from the Greek *entheos* meaning 'the God within.' Back in the eighteenth century, enthusiasm was often regarded with suspicion, perhaps as possession of evil spirits or hysteria. But, although critics aimed to be derogatory in using the term "enthusiasts," Wesley was seeking to recover something vital that was in danger of being lost from the Christian faith. As American United Methodist minister and author, Paul Chilcote notes: "The Wesleys rediscovered this important spiritual law: the church needs enthused disciples. 'Enthused' literally means to be properly filled with God."[97]

As we look at ourselves today, it can be argued that we seem to have developed something of an issue with being zealous! Wesley saw in his day that the Church of England he was ordained into was largely failing to reach people with the life transforming Gospel. Tragically, we can see that this is now the plight of our beloved Methodist Church.

Of course, there is an appropriate caution to carry about zeal. Throughout history people have been zealous about all sorts of things that have been plainly wrong or horribly destructive. Even within the church, there have been too many instances when people have been altogether zealous about things that did not really matter! It is all too easy to sometimes exhaust our zeal on side issues, or even errors, rather than in fulfilling God's central calling. Wesley himself was well-aware of the potential dangers of religious zeal. In his 1781 Sermon 92, 'On Zeal', he noted that: "nothing has done more disservice to religion, or more mischief to mankind, than a sort of zeal which has for several ages prevailed, both in pagan, Mahometan (Muslim) and Christian nations." And yet he also maintained that "without zeal it is impossible either to make any considerable progress in religion ourselves, or to do any considerable service to our neighbour, whether in temporal or spiritual things."

We should not be surprised that the initial zeal has been hard to maintain. For instance, German sociologist Max Weber's principle of "routinisation" is well documented.

As Meadows puts it: "This theory posits the inevitable change of character in social movements as they are transmuted from charismatic organisations into settled institutions. In short, the charismatic vitality with which a movement first sets out is channelled into institutional structures and eventually gets lost. Flexible structures put in place by the first generation to organise and serve a growing movement, become the hardened objects of preservation by subsequent generations. From a theological perspective, it can describe how the church ends up having the form of religion without the power of godliness; and it is not difficult to see how this process can account for the decline of Methodism as an ecclesiastical institution. Ironically, formalism in the Church of England was the very problem that the early Methodist movement sought to address."[98]

However, I take great heart from recalling the words of Anglican minister John Stott: "We do not need to wait for the Holy Spirit to come: He (sic) came on the day of Pentecost. He has never left the church." Indeed so. What we lack is not the Holy Spirit. We see the Spirit at work in many quarters. But what we do too often lack is the zeal which releases the Spirit and enables us once again to be a passionately missional, discipling movement.

Lesslie Newbigin, the notable author and bishop in the Church of South India, compared Pentecost with the striking of oil. When a powerful flow of oil is achieved, there is a lot of excitement and action. It is a big, extravagant (and potentially dangerous) moment. It is cause for uninhibited celebration — a wild scene. But it is the result that really matters. It must be tamed and delivered to where it is needed. Unless the well is capped and the oil directed through pipes, the fuss is worth nothing. The pipes running across the land look boring compared with the scene when the oil first flowed free. But that is where the whole event becomes fruitful. It would be infantile to want to recreate the excitement of the day when oil was first struck. If the oil can be disciplined for the wellbeing of humanity, the strike is worth it.

This was surely the remarkable gift – and legacy – of Wesley: a Godly zeal that both reached whole swathes of society with the love of God and also provided the energy to form and shape the patterns that ensured people could grow in grace.

It was anthropologist Margaret Mead who famously said: "Never doubt that a small group of thoughtful, committed citizens can change the world; indeed, it's the only thing that ever has." The growth of the Methodist movement in the eighteenth century is dynamic proof of this statement. A growing vibrant network of small groups of people up and down the land all set about changing their world and together created a fire across much of the nation.

It is this that I long to see in our beloved Methodism. As God's Holy Spirit is with us, and moves us towards a new future, I pray for a renewed Godly zeal to be our hallmark. Why? So that we might once again face ridicule for the passionate way in which we live, for the way that God's love has so taken hold of us that we are doing what feels "vile," — that we are prepared to let go of so much, so that those who might not otherwise be touched with God's love would be so reached. All with "unfaltering resolve."

It is of paramount importance to recognise just how fully lay leadership was a vital and key part of the mobilisation of the early Methodist movement.

Chapter 10
Mobilising Effective Leadership

The rapid growth of early Methodism was a stunning and God-inspired combination of both an openness to the work of the Holy Spirit, a zealous commitment to preaching and living out the Good News of the Gospel AND a development of structures and methods that enabled and accelerated the work of God. This was a key part of the genius of John Wesley. As British Methodist Minister and Moderator of the Free Churches Group, Helen Cameron puts it, "for Wesley, a heart overflowing with God's love was always represented by a governed and disciplined and ordered life."[99] This was about both everyone's individual walk with God (defined as being part of the "people called Methodists") and the developing life of the connexion.

Having a clarity of message and a passion to share that message carries no guarantee that a long-term growing, flourishing, society-transforming movement will develop. This became abundantly clear to Wesley. On fire, fuelled by his deepening response to the continuing gift of God's grace, Wesley was enduringly compelled by his "why": the vision of the transformation of the land and the renewal of the church. His zeal drew many towards him and, much more importantly, beyond him into a living, transformative relationship with God. Beyond that, critically, through the years of his extraordinary ministry Wesley also developed methods to enable the movement to sustain its growth and stay true to its why. He did this through a pragmatic and dynamic mixture of maintaining both flexibility and control and of holding and releasing authority and responsibility. He thus empowered many people as they were found by God's grace to join the movement, to discover fresh vocation, realise leadership potential and embody the Methodist cause.

It is well documented that Wesley found the example of fellow evangelist George Whitfield – preaching in the open air to vast crowds – shocking and "vile." Nevertheless, ever the pragmatist, he was prepared to change his mind upon observing the fruits of Whitefield's preaching. So it was that in March 1739 Wesley first preached outdoors. By September that year, he was preaching to extraordinarily large crowds of sometimes up to 20,000.

Ordinary people were less likely to be attending established church, so Wesley went to them. The very mixed reception with which he was met is vividly described in his journals but plentiful were the times when he was gladly received.

As previously noted, it quickly became clear to Wesley that field preaching – however effective it was – could not be the only method to fulfil his mission. In her thesis on the development of early circuits, British Methodist Minister, Christine Pocock observes that: "as he itinerated around the country, Wesley recognised that if those who responded to his preaching were not brought into a society they ... 'grew faint in their minds, and fell back into what they were before'... He therefore combined itinerant preaching with establishing societies in which those newly converted could be spiritually and pastorally nurtured."[100]

As Wesley himself noted in the minutes of the 1748 Conference: "Almost all the seed has fallen by the wayside; there is scarce any fruit of it remaining." Without good nurture and oversight, awakened souls could not 'watch over one another in love' and believers could not 'build up one another and bear one another's burdens.'"

With great pragmatism, therefore, Wesley explored, adopted and adapted a range of methods to serve the growing movement. These came to include field preaching, classes, bands, societies, circuits, itinerant 'ministers,' annual conferences and publications. Gradually all of this was synthesised into a consistent whole that became characteristic of Methodism. Every part was instituted and maintained with the sole and clear aim of enabling the movement to flourish – ever seeking to fulfil the central why. As I noted earlier, all of these parts could be regarded as a network of "spaces for grace", enabling people to grow in holiness. The structures were only there to support the mission. Wesley experimented, tested and refined the methods so the movement could expand but – most importantly – still remain focused as it gradually moved beyond his direct control.

With regard to the status of the developing movement, also as previously noted, Wesley regarded Methodism as 'ecclesiola in ecclesia,' (a church within the church), and maintained a life-long hope that Methodism could stay within the Church of England and therefore under, and within, its overall episcopal oversight. He came to regard himself as a 'scriptural episkopos'[101] with an episcopal (overseeing) role that sat, albeit increasingly uncomfortably, alongside the continuing role of the parochial clergy in offering episkope to the "people called Methodists."

As Atkins puts it, "the initial 'structures' of Methodism were those which encouraged and enabled people to become better disciples of Jesus. That's chiefly why they are as they are."[102] Crucially, as he goes on to note, those early structures – societies, classes and bands – were lay-led.

Appreciating the Vital Ministry of Lay Leaders

We therefore start to observe something very significant about how "the people called Methodists" were mobilised: through the raising up of local, contextual and incarnational lay leadership and also the development of good oversight focused on enabling that local lay leadership to be as effective as possible. "Wesley trained and mobilised a massive army of leaders, putting as many as one in ten of his members into leadership roles – people of all walks of life."[103]

As Sweet puts it so plainly: "One of the most revolutionary features of the Wesleyan revival was its liberation of the laity for leadership and its blurring of the lines between clergy and lay when it came to priestly functions and spiritual guides. Wesley didn't worry about qualifications since he trusted on-the-job training and expected all Methodists to be lifelong learners. Growth in theological depth and priestly skills was what it meant to be a Methodist."[104]

Atkins reflects: "In spite of the fact that the Wesleys and a few ordained clergy exercised leadership in Methodism, the great majority of preachers and society and class leaders were laypeople. It's not without reason that many refer to Methodism as a 'lay movement.' There was certainly leadership and authority, but of a kind that assumed that disciples could and should minister to each other for the benefit of all ... the societies themselves – as the very term suggests – relied heavily upon what is now sometimes described as 'every member ministry.'"[105]

We have already noted how Wesley's vision was a rediscovery of a sense of movement and impulse seen in the early church. It has been observed that such renewals always seem to be founded upon a raising up and release of lay leadership. As American Professor of evangelism, George Hunter III notes: "The identity of the church is located in its apostolic mission and ministry to people (and to the whole population) who are not yet people of faith, and this ministry and mission are primarily entrusted to the laity."[106] So it was in the case of the rapid growth of the Wesley-an patterns of mission and discipleship. American scholar and author, Winfield Bevins, puts it like this: "It was this vision of empowering ordinary, non-ordained people for God's mission that was at the heart of the Wesleyan revival."[107]

As we look at our current patterns of being "the people called Methodists" I think it is important to emphasise that this vision was not about finding people to support the developing movement's structures but about inspiring, equipping and releasing everyone involved to play their part in fulfilling the why of the movement.

The role of class leader emerged as a vital lay leadership role in the Methodist movement's development. They provide a particularly inspiring exemplar to us today. It is helpful to spend some time exploring their place within the growing movement, together with reflection as to their subsequent costly demise and, with it, the withering of effective local lay missional and discipling leadership.

The class leaders became the backbone of the emerging growing movement. They offered a consistent spiritual guide and accompaniment through direct weekly contact with those within their care. The genius of this model was that people's continuing response to God's "waves of grace" was enmeshed within the developing practice of growing through the "means of grace." Personal holiness was deepened through the experience of growing in social holiness within the class, thereby encouraging the fulfilment of the movement's why of spreading scriptural holiness. Early Methodism enabled an explosion of this missional, disciple-growing lay leadership held within appropriate oversight and accountability. This provided the nimble structure that in turn fuelled incarnational, locally rooted mission and ministry which proceeded to transform lives, communities and even, remarkably, arguably turned the nation away from civil war.

So it was that the network of class leaders enabled every member, and seeker, in every part of the land to benefit from local, indigenous missional, discipling leadership. In recognising the importance of this within the emerging contemporary scene within the Church of England, Anglican Priest and author, Malcolm Grundy references Roland Allen, missionary to China in the early twentieth century, who powerfully argues of the need for local indigenous leadership to have missional and discipling effectiveness within different cultural contexts.[108]

As the early Methodist movement developed, class leaders took their place alongside a developing itinerant order of Wesley's assistants and helpers, who then gradually began to take on the role that was in time to become referred to as ministers and, more recently, as "presbyters." Without class leaders it seems reasonable to say that the itinerant ministry could not have developed and thrived. The significance of this dynamic relationship has perhaps been too often overlooked. As Pocock notes in her exploration of the development of circuits, "the extent to which the itinerant system depended on the quality and commitment of local leadership is noted as an under-researched area."[109]

This is deeply significant. It seems to me that the effective interlinking and interlocking of local lay leadership within the wider movement as a whole — as a connexion — was a significant part of the genius of the emerging movement. It provided an intricately balanced pattern of oversight which enabled both rich diversity and galvanising unity. This characteristic, if not unique, pattern of oversight of "the people called Methodists" is worth considering further — through the lens of "episkope" (oversight).

Looking at Leadership and Ministry through the Lens of Oversight – "Episkope"

Episkope is often described, within the Methodist world at least, as "watching over in love" and also referred to — engagingly and helpfully — as "keeping an eye on what is happening."[110] Although there is more to embrace within a fuller understanding of the practice of episkope, these descriptions provide a good starting point, particularly in reflecting upon the ministry of oversight offered within the early Methodist movement (whilst, of course, at that time other spiritual oversight continued to be available within the Parish system).

Episkope was, and always is, a vital thread in the tapestry of maintaining and developing long-term sustainable and healthy Christian mission and ministry. It lies at the heart of what it is to be a covenant people.[111] Far too many and frequent are the disheartening stories of churches and ministries where that oversight has not been appropriately and effectively offered and/or received. Without good balanced oversight, ministry and mission suffers. All too often there is a misunderstanding of episkope which has leaned either towards overbearing control or virtual abandonment.

As already noted, it is of paramount importance to recognise just how fully lay leadership was a vital and key part of the mobilisation of the early Methodist movement. Lay leaders were at the core of the raising up of "the people called Methodists." They were distinctively entrusted with their own particular role of oversight (episkope). They were released as fully-fledged leaders in their own right. Class leaders, therefore, offered an inspiring example of lay "personal episkope" which encouraged them to grow in personal and social holiness and thereby play their part in fulfilling the calling of Methodism. Lay leaders were a countervailing expression of episkope to Wesley's own personal episcopal reach. He recognised this layer of lay personal episkope to be an essential part of the oversight necessary to enable the Methodist movement to pursue its calling.[112]

Crucially, though, they too were also supported and held in good oversight. So, we can observe that the developing Methodist episkope was established through a distinctive inter-locking and dynamic combination of class leaders, helpers and assistants as well as Wesley himself. It encouraged local indigenous mission and discipleship to flourish within a held-together-in-connexion cohesiveness. (All of this, as already noted, was held – increasingly uncomfortably – within the "big church", throughout Wesley's lifetime.).

Atkins, helpfully, emphasises the significance of these fast-growing societies and their classes not becoming independent, free-standing groups: "They were connected together in significant ways. Initially this came through the ministry of John Wesley himself. To be a Methodist society meant being 'in connexion' with Mr Wesley ... However ... Wesley couldn't be everywhere at once and 'travelling preachers' arrived to share the work almost from the start."[113] These travelling preachers served and helped to lead a number of societies and, from these, developed 'circuits.' Circuits in turn "provided coordination, enabling structures, resources and mutual encouragement for a burgeoning disciple-making movement."[114]

Arguably, one of the most distinctive features and hallmarks of this pristine model of Methodist episkope, which gives potent life to being in connexion, is the multi-layered and interlocking oversight of visitation. The 1988 Methodist report, The Ministry of the People of God, explores the significance of this aspect of oversight: "In the Biblical tradition the verb 'to visit' characteristically describes God's looking up individuals or the people with a concern for their welfare. His visitation was focused in Jesus ... The ministry of visitation to churches is practised by a leader (or a team of leaders) visiting a church from outside to bring a fresh and critical perspective to its understanding of its life and work."[115]

Perhaps this practice of visitation most vividly and practically embodies that function of episkope which is about "watching over in love" and "keeping any eye on what is happening"):

- Class leaders offered this episkope in every place and context, the class meeting being the sinew of early Methodism[116] (In the early days, class leaders would actually visit members in their homes each week, but this adjusted to the visitation being by way of the weekly class meeting.).

- Assistants and helpers began (in the first instance almost as extensions of Wesley himself) to provide an episkope of visitation to classes (and societies), set aside as they were to a "local translocal"[117] itinerant ministry within circuits.[118] They were regarded by Wesley as "extraordinary messengers," and his hope (ultimately unfulfilled, of course) was that a spiritual renewal of the "ordinary messengers" (Anglican clergy) would render them unnecessary in the longer term.[119] The "translocal" dimension is very important: it is the ability to take a larger, bird's-eye view of an area and the mission and ministry already in hand and the potential for new and fresh mission. The opportunity and potential for this translocal oversight is well-founded within circuits, so long as the role of those with that responsibility do not become too involved in the local.

- Wesley himself continued to offer a personal "scriptural episkopos", thereby embodying a focus for every part of the movement being in connexion. In time, this became held by the Conference, ultimately as successor to Wesley, in providing the over-arching unifying "corporate episkope" of responding to the work of God around the Connexion and providing the corporate episcopal oversight. The offices of President and Vice-President of the Conference came to embody the oversight of "connexional visitation" to circuits.

Though the significant lay leadership and ministry role of class leader is still embedded within Methodism's 'Constitution, Practice and Discipline' as a vital part of the church's oversight, it − or anything like it − is in practice far less significant today and the notion of true *lay* personal episkope has very substantially withered. I contend that this has had a huge impact on the ability of Methodism to both raise up and then (even more significantly) sustain missionally diverse and contextually relevant expressions of mission. As a consequence, I would argue that:

- the overall distinctive episkope of the Methodist Church has become unbalanced and unable to effectively fulfil its function of missional and pastoral oversight,

- the potential for large-scale, naturally developing, indigenous local missional development is hindered,

- the value and potential arising from being "a connexion" are weakened.

The Cost of What We Have Lost

As I say, I argue that a critically significant hole has emerged within the rich and distinctive model of multi-interlocking Methodist episkope. It is the incalculable loss of the empowering, equipping and releasing of the lay leadership role embodied, as its clearest historic example, in the office of the class leader.[120]

There is an important and complex story as to why that hole has been allowed to, and at times encouraged to, develop. Some of that story is simply about power struggles and jockeying for position and influence. This began early on within the movement, as the ministry of helpers and assistants grew in significance.[121] In part it developed out of the gradual developing of the Methodist Church as a Church and the taking on by ministers of those aspects of the episkope role that through Wesley's lifetime had remained with parochial clergy. In the taking on those aspects, ministers also came to take on the episkope which had been the responsibility of the lay. It is also perhaps linked with ecumenical developments which have aligned the role of Methodist ministers (now presbyters and deacons) more closely to, in particular, Anglican counterparts (I think it is hard for us today to recognise how distinctive the early models of Methodist ministry were as compared to Anglican clergy.) It is also clear from the range of relevant Methodist reports produced over the last thirty years that personal episkope has become regarded now as limited to the ordained.[122]

The 1982 World Council of Churches landmark 'Baptism, Eucharist and Ministry' report[123] helps us to recognise and understand more clearly the consequences of the loss of the personal episkope role of the class leader by considering the three dimensions of good episkope that it highlights as essential: personal, collegial and communal.

Contemporary Methodism has well-established patterns of communal episkope at every level (Conference, District Synod, Circuit Meeting, Church Council, Pastoral Committee). There is good collegial episkope amongst presbyters and deacons, and to an extent amongst local preachers. Personal episkope is also evident through the ordained roles of President, District Chair, superintendents and presbyters.

However, as noted above, the personal episkope of the class leader — such a distinctive and missionally significant part of the early Connexional episkope — has practically faded away. Though lay people continue to play an important part in the communal episkope of the church, it is, I contend, not possible for an episkope role to be fully embodied and effective without all three aspects — personal, collegial and communal — being in place. An order of episkope cannot fully contribute to communal episkope if it does not have a clear personal — and then also collegial — episkope aspect.

The absence of the meaningful personal (and collegial)[124] lay episkope leads to:

- the absence of effective and dynamic local episkope which regularly reaches (and watches over) every member (and seeker),

- the "local translocal" (set apart) episkope of circuit presbyters and deacons being overtaken by an embedded focus and activity within the heart of local church life.[125] This has fatally debilitated the episkope of ministerial visitation (to churches, local missional communities and discipling groups) which was a vital part of the role[126] and

- the genius of indigenous local mission and discipleship held together in full connexion as an effective movement is lost because the essential episkope-reach right into the grassroots is simply not there.

This has consequences for every part of the connexion as the personal, collegial and communal episkope role of the lay (as embodied historically in the class leader) could and should necessarily play its part in shaping every aspect of the Church's life.

The intentional, and positively much fuller inclusion of the lay within decision-making since the days of Wesley, has been more than an off-set in its effectiveness by the demise of the full-blooded personal, local lay episkope embodied, historically, in the class leader.

Re-Mobilising the Lay Leadership of the Movement

The re-imagination and reinvigoration of the personal (and hence fully-enabled collegial and communal) episkope of local lay leadership has the potential to rekindle the renewing of the work of God within the Methodist movement. The recent development of the Local Lay Pastor office offers some movement in what I would hope is the right direction, and yet, as I have sought to set out, that office still falls a good deal short of the richness of the early days of the movement.

In rediscovering this distinctively Methodist lay missional and discipling leadership role, a deeper understanding and appreciation of the connexion can be envisaged, through:

- a new commitment to genuinely raising up local indigenous leaders in mission and discipleship,

- the rediscovery of the distinctive and liberating role of ordained ministry as offering a vital set apart, local translocal episkope,

- and the creative weaving together of:

    - local, 'translocal' and connexional,

    - lay and ordained,

    - indigenous and set apart.

Steven Croft, the Bishop of Oxford, exploring contemporary challenges for ministry within the Church of England, powerfully argues that we continue to need healthy models of lay and ordained leadership for flourishing blended ecologies: "Local clergy overseeing inherited congregations and networks of fresh expressions need to understand themselves again as quasi-bishops, whose role is to equip the whole people of God to be missionaries in the fields."[127]

Theologically and ecclesiologically, such a re-awakening could enable "the people called Methodists" to freshly explore and model how our Connexion can more fully and dynamically reflect the "perichoresis" that is the "circle dance of the trinitarian life" within the Godhead.[128]

Missiologically, and crucially to the thrust of so much of this book, it could enable us to truly embrace and encourage a rich blended ecology of inherited church and emerging fresh expressions — all held together and thriving through the glorious strength of being "in connexion."

REVIVE US AGAIN

It is time for "the people called Methodists" to recognise that we have become lumbered with all kinds of things (nearly always with the very best of intentions) which don't really fit and aren't true to who we really are.

Chapter 11

Rejuvenating a Movement of Transformation

I have covered much ground in sharing how I was inspired through my personal sabbatical journey as to how our story of origin could shape our future. I have tried to set out the deepening convictions of my heart as they developed and grew. My sincere hope is that what I have written might stimulate wider conversation and debate and encourage "the people called Methodists" to re-discover valuable treasures all too long overlooked. I furthermore hope that it might open up a future journey which has less anxiety and introspection about identity and purpose (and worse still, survival) and has instead a reinvigorating inspiration founded on a recovery of confidence in our "divinely appointed mission."

In 1 Samuel 17 we see the boy, David, lumbered by the imposition of all the weight of Saul's armour as he is prepared to face the giant. The thinking was sound enough: Surely David should need what anyone else would have to fight the enemy? However, it completely ill-fitted him. It wasn't consistent with who he was. He needed to be freed of what had been put upon him so that he could be who he really was and thereby could fulfil his mission using the tools and resources (in his case sling and stones) that were authentically his.

I want to suggest it is time for "the people called Methodists" to recognise that we have become lumbered with all kinds of things (nearly always with the very best of intentions) which don't really fit and aren't true to who we really are. Their impact has come to hinder us from fulfilling God's mission.

How might all of this actually shape up in a new way of being? Surely this could be such an exciting and God-inspired adventure. To be clear, the last thing I have in mind is to embark on a laborious process of re-writing Standing Orders or opening up new avenues of debate about our constitutional structures. Paradoxically, I would want to maintain that a good deal of what remains embedded in our Standing Orders naturally tends to support much of what I have set out.

Rather, I would hope that we might cultivate some fresh space ("spaces for grace") at all levels of our connexion — of our being together in all our diverse ways — to receive fresh inspiration and energy to:

- discover confidence in our founding and identifying calling and determining priority as agents of spiritual and social transformation,

- be renewed in our appreciation of the stupendous love of God as we know it in Jesus and the boundless reach and power of the Gospel,

- appreciate afresh the essential hallmarks of our being as growing in dazzling holiness and captivating grace,

- recognise God's working in all things for good in raising up the opportunity for us to grow as a blended ecology and a movement/church,

- embrace the creative potential for our "with-ness" as a connexion to be liberating and mobilising for all kinds of diverse mission and ministry in every corner of our land,

- contribute and partner with our sister churches with humility and yet confidence, being agents of renewal: influential yeast in the mix,

- hold less tightly to our inherited being, with a faith-filled appetite to share ourselves freely, passionately, trusting in Jesus' words in Matthew 16:25, that as we lose our life for Christ we will find it and

- explore again how we can truly mobilise lay leaders, supported by distinctive oversight which enables that lay leadership to flourish in a myriad of places and ways.

I believe now is a kairos opportunity to shift the balance of our self-understanding and ordering towards affirming our best identity as a movement/church:

- I see it as being there in our very DNA (and indeed in our Standing Orders). At one level I think we can't fight it (and we make ourselves ill at ease with ourselves as we resist).

- I observe that the needs of our society and wider world echo so clearly the needs that the early Methodist movement faced and we need to liberate ourselves afresh so that we can fulfil our founding calling to offer the spiritual and social transformation that Christ offers with passion and energy.

- I think that the progress and developments of the Fresh Expressions movement should both hearten and challenge us about the way it chimes with our early missional movement. By releasing our movement's energy we can, I believe, join in even more effectively with the move of God's Spirit in and through the Fresh Expressions movement.

As I say, in all I have written, I have purposefully resisted talking much about structures. Of course they matter but, as we have already seen, at its best Methodism has always regarded its structures as servants of the mission. The danger remains, despite recent efforts, that the structures too often feel like the master rather than the servant.

To refer back to 'Called to Love and Praise,' it noted that a distinctive emphasis of the Methodist Church is "the conviction that the Church should be structured for mission and able to respond pragmatically, when new needs or opportunities arise."[129] It develops this point by saying, "the Methodist Church, pointing to its own origins, and to Scripture, holds to the conviction that the Holy Spirit leads the Church to adapt its structures as it faces new situations and challenges. This flexibility is itself an important principle, rooted in scripture, theology and experience. Methodists, therefore, should not feel the need resolutely to defend the structures of the Methodist Church."[130]

With commendable insight it adds: "But there are challenges to be faced and warnings to be heeded. Here three in particular may be mentioned. First, Methodist origins invite the question whether the Church's structures help its members to grow in holiness. If the class meeting has largely gone, what has taken its place? Second, the Methodist Church, like others, faces the danger of becoming ponderous and inflexible; structures adapted to one missionary situation become perpetuated as hindrances to missionary activity in another. Third, in replacing those structures, there is the danger of being guided exclusively by the pastoral needs of settled congregations turned in on themselves."[131]

So, in creating "space for grace" – for renewal – there does need to be a simplifying of structures. My quietness about such things within this book so far is based on my conviction that it is only as and when we really grasp hold of our core identity and purpose with renewed confidence that we will find the courage to truly and radically re-shape the structures to (once again?) be "good and faithful servants" of God's mission.

The clues, though, of how re-shaping of structures might begin to look are evident I think:

- Taking seriously what Conference reports have repeatedly acknowledged in recent years — that the circuit is well placed to be the "primary unit of mission."

- As such, the circuit can be an effective "container" for all kinds of different missional enterprises and forms; a blended ecology of inherited and new, gathered and dispersed.

- Recognising in turn that the currently required infrastructure that comes from being constituted and operating as a Local Church (within our Standing Orders) can all too often stifle missional and discipling energy rather than release it. Instead, there needs to be a radical re-focussing towards prioritising smaller (primarily lay-led) gatherings (spaces for grace) of all kinds of shape, size and missional and discipling intention. This needs to be in tandem with a shift away from viewing the inherited assumptions of the Local Church (and in particular the focus on, typically, Sunday morning attendance in an owned building) as being the normative, "proper" or "most effective" expression of Methodist presence and activity and mission.

- Circuits can become more effective in ensuring that all that rightly needs to be in place (in fulfilling the laws of the land, in safeguarding and in administrative excellence) is professionally provided. This includes, it seems to me, a fairly radical approach to trusteeship, which releases most members from the burden of managing trusteeship and re-entrusts those equipped and called to fulfil that role effectively. (In this we perhaps recognise a helpful analogy in Acts 6:1-6, with the calling of people to specific roles in order to release others to fulfil their vocation.).

- The circuit — as our Standing Orders have always maintained — is the ecclesial place in which ministerial oversight is held, so that this vital translocal role of oversight over diverse ecclesial and missional communities can be exercised with integrity and due attention, without ministers being so embedded in the local as has become the case. (It is interesting to note, in passing, that Methodist Standing Orders know nothing of "sections," which have become so commonplace in practice. That is but one example of the way in which the church has moved to a model of deep-embedding of ministers within the local contexts at the cost, as I have already argued, of their vital role of oversight.).

A re-framing of structures in anything like this way could be quite radical to our current patterns, even though it would represent something of a re-creation of what was in place when the Methodist movement was growing strongly in its early years. As an example, in 1765 the York Circuit was formed: three ministers had oversight covering an area that included Scarborough and Tadcaster.[132] A further example is to remember an early stage of the movement's development when there were (just) seven circuits — London, Bristol, Evesham, Yorkshire (which included six other counties, Newcastle and Wales). Their task was "to administer the spiritual feeding, teaching and guidance of the Methodist people."[133]

It seems to me that the profoundly different models and structures of ministry that we see in the early, rapidly growing phase of the Methodist movement offer us an exciting pattern to be re-imagined for today: hugely diverse expressions of mission and ministry, with considerably simplified patterns of local ecclesiology, flourishing through the equipping and releasing of local lay pastors, entrepreneurs, pioneers, all overseen, supported and encouraged through re-energised models of translocal — circuit — oversight.

The Conference Report of 2008, 'The Missional Nature of the Circuit,' helpfully explores the way in which circuits can oversee fresh expressions, noting that "it may be the role of the circuit to resource and manage fresh expressions rather than local churches — for a circuit to decide together how it can respond to local or context-based missional needs and develop the ministry of the circuit in appropriate ways. This could be in the form of new congregations or classes, networks, meeting places, training programmes or practical expressions of mission, or the releasing of presbyters from maintaining traditional work in 'sections' or settled congregations."[134]

In addition, I return to the desire to look at the church from the other way up. Remember, a core element of our why is to "spread scriptural holiness through the land." From our earliest days there was a grand and ambitious view of the "world as our parish", with a commitment to be fulfilling our mission through the personal response of individuals, growing in social holiness.

If we are truly to embrace a vision of being in connexion, which is much more about truly releasing and establishing the growth of an extraordinary diversity of mission and ministry around the whole nation, there is a case to be made for as much energy, resource and trust to be directed to the local. The centre then needs to become as nimble and light as possible, focusing on only that which is absolutely essential to support the movement's health and growth.

But as I say, I think we will only ever happily embrace radically simpler, more apt and appropriate structures once we are sensing a re-vitalisation in our intrinsic identity and purpose. That is the vital "next step."

In conclusion, I return to Beck's inspiring writing. He quotes a colleague in recognising that there are primarily three possible paths through which a church can experience revitalisation.

1. Re-engineering: Looking at all the parts of church life and developing a new strategy, or re-organisation, to make the current version its best version.

2. Revival: That occurs through the powerful outpouring of the Holy Spirit. This is, of course, something we pray for and can happen but we can't predict or plan for it. We pray and wait – and it is important that we do so, far more than we usually do these days.

3. Re-Missioning: By focusing on the Great Commission, the church is re-orientated towards becoming a mission movement. Where re-engineering begins with the church, re-missioning begins with the mission. In re-engineering the church sets the agenda, in re-missioning the mission context sets the agenda."[135]

My hope is that we might explore how we can focus on "re-missioning" rather than "re-engineering" whilst taking seriously our need, as part of our mission, to pray and wait on God for revival. As Beck so helpfully puts it: "To try and catalyse revitalisation with better organisational leadership and the introduction of new programmes is not effective. Resurrection cannot be programmed, managed or owned."[136]

I close with some words of Professor Clive Marsh, presently Principal of the Queen's Foundation, Birmingham. When I read them they warmed my heart and deepened my hopefulness and confidence in all that "the people called Methodists" could and should be in the twenty-first century: "Methodism as a movement and at its best, is passionate evangelism wedded to a burning zeal for social action ... If Methodism did not exist, it would have to be invented. The dynamic combination of Christian social action and intelligent evangelism is arguably a uniquely concentrated ecclesial embodiment within a social denomination."[137]

So it is, that my looking back to our origins has inspired me deeply to see what, with fresh imagination and resilient courage, could re-mission "the people called Methodists" in this twenty-first century to contribute significantly to the spiritual and social transformation of the nation and the renewing of the Church at large.

I pray that this book might play a part in enabling that to be our future.

About the Author

Born and raised in Lancaster, Leslie studied accountancy and law at University before training and qualifying as a Chartered Accountant. His local Methodist Church, in Torrisholme, Morecambe, nurtured his faith. Through the years, they encouraged him to grow and develop by way of welcoming and encouraging his contributions through music, youth work and later in preaching.

Leslie was accepted for the Methodist Ministry in 1995 and met his wife, Gill, at Wesley College, Bristol, where they both trained. They were married in 1996 and became parents to Laura in 2000. Prior to becoming Chair of the Yorkshire North and East District in 2017, Leslie has served in circuit ministry in Barnsley, Stockport and York.

Leslie is currently co-Chair of the Methodist Church's New Places for New People Guiding Team and serves as a Trustee of Fresh Expressions Ltd.

References

[1] A recording of this hymn to the tune I wrote on sabbatical, *Lilly*, can be found here; kindly recorded by the choir of Northallerton Methodist Church: https://youtu.be/m06yBesDDLo

[2] John Wesley wrote his "A Plain Account of the People Called Methodists" in 1748 and the title has been commonly used over the years.

[3] Methodist Church in Britain, *'Called to Love and Praise,'* (https://www.methodist.org.uk/media/1993/fo-statement-called-to-love-and-praise-1999.pdf, 1999) (para. 5.1).

[4] Howcroft, K. 2014. (Online) https://www.methodist.org.uk/about-us/news/latest-news/all-news/back-to-the-bible-forward-to-the-world-inaugural-address-of-the-methodist-president/

[5] In particular, within the Methodist Church in Britain's 'Constitutional Practice and Discipline' https://www.methodist.org.uk/for-churches/governance/cpd/

[6] Quoted by Beck, Michael. *Deep roots, Wild Branches: Revitalising the Church in the Blended Ecology,* (Franklin: Seedbed Publishing, 2019), (p. xvi).

[7] Sweet, L. 2012. *The Greatest Story Never Told.* (Nashville: Abingdon Press).

[8] Sinek, S. 2009. *Start With Why.* (London: Penguin Books).

[9] Methodist Church in Britain. 2018. *Reaffirming Our Calling: Strategic Developments.* (Online). https://www.methodist.org.uk/media/5888/counc_mc18-1_reaffirming_our_-calling_jan_2018.pdf (para. 1).

[10] Ibid, para. 3ff.

[11] Ibid, para. 10.

[12] Sinek. *Start With Why.* (p. 213).

[13] Sinek. *Start With Why.* (pp. 214-215).

[14] Heath, E. 2016. *God Unbound: Wisdom from Galatians for the Anxious Church.* (Nashville: Upper Room Books) (p. 28).

[15] https://www.methodist.org.uk/for-churches/governance/cpd/ (p. 72).

[16] https://www.methodist.org.uk/media/26649/conf-2022-cpd-vol-2.pdf (p. 213).

[17] '*The Second Quinquennial Report (2013) of the Joint Implementation Commission under the Covenant between The Methodist Church of Great Britain And The Church of England*' *(http://www.anglican-methodist.org.uk/wp-content/uploads/2017/12/JIC-2013-Challenge-of-the-Covenant.pdf* (p. 6).

[18] Sweet. *The Greatest Story Never Told.* (p. xviii).

[19] Howcroft. 2014. (Online). https://www.methodist.org.uk/about-us/news/latest-news/all-news/back-to-the-bible-forward-to-the-world-inaugural-address-of-the-methodist-president/

[20] ibid, p. Xvi.

[21] Sangster, WE. 1938. *Methodism can be born again.* (London: Hodder and Stoughton).

[22] Ibid, p. 36.

[23] Ibid, p. 37.

[24] Methodist Church in Britain. '*Called to Love and Praise.*' (para. 5.2).

[25] Beck, M. 2020. *A Field Guide to Methodist Fresh Expressions.* (Nashville: Abingdon Press). (p. 29).

[26] Wesley, J. 1745. *Works Vol VIII, A Farther Appeal to Men of Reason and Religion.* (p. 112).

[27] Sweet. *The Greatest Story Never Told*. (p. 56).

[28] Beck. *A Field Guide to Methodist Fresh Expressions.* (p. 40).

[29] Meadows, P. 2013. *Wesleyan DNA of Discipleship.* (Cambridge: Grove Books). (p. 5).

[30] From a sermon preached by Ruth Etchells, quoted in: Samuel, Calvin, *More Distinct: Reclaiming holiness for the world today*, (London: IVP, 2018) (p. 2).

[31] Ibid, p. 3.

[32] *'The Great Privilege of Those That Are Born of God,'* which Wesley preached on 30 May 1731.

[33] Howcroft. 2014. (Online). www.methodist.org.uk/news-and-events/news-releases/back-tothe-

bible-forward-to-the-world-inaugural-address-of-the-methodist-president.

[34] Heath, E & Kisker, S. 2011. *Longing for Spring: A new vision for Wesleyan Community* (Oregon: Cascade Books). (p. 37).

[35] Methodist Church in Britain, *'Called to Love and Praise'* par 4.2.2.

[36] Knight, H. (Online) https://www.catalystresources.org/consider-wesley-37/ (accessed 30/5/23).

[37] Heath & Scott, *Longing for Spring: A new vision for Wesleyan Community.* (p. 41).

[38] Wesley, J. 1742. "The Character of a Methodist" quoted in *'The Bicentennial Edition of the Works of John Wesley'* (Nashville: Abingdon Press, 2005), Vol: 9:35.

[39] Ibid, Vol: 9:41.

[40] Teal, Richard quoted in https://www.methodist.org.uk/about-us/news/the-president-and-vice-president-of-the-conference/the-blog-of-the-president-and-vice-president-of-conference/personal-holiness/ (accessed 30/5/23).

[41] John Wesley's 'A Plain Account of the People called Methodists' quoted at https://jamespedlar.ca/2011/09/22/john-wesley-and-the-mission-of-god-part-5-social-holiness/ (accessed 30/5/23).

[42] Teal, Richard https://www.methodist.org.uk/about-us/news/the-president-and-vice-president-of-the-conference/the-blog-of-the-president-and-vice-president-of-conference/social-holiness/

[43] https://www.methodist.org.uk/about-us/news/the-president-and-vice-president-of-the-conference/the-blog-of-the-president-and-vice-president-of-conference/social-holiness/ (accessed 17/5/21)

[44] Heath. *God Unbound,* (p. 37).

[45] Yancey, P. 1997. *What's So Amazing About Grace*, (Grand Rapids, Zondervan). (p. 45).

[46] Wesley, J. 1740. Quotes from *Sermon 128, Free Grace'* preached at Bristol.

[47] Affirming that we've recognised that personal and social holiness are a vital part of that.

[48] Carder, K. 2016. *A Wesleyan Understanding of Grace.* (Online). https://www.resourceumc.org/en/content/a-wesleyan-understanding-of-grace (accessed 30/5/23).

[49] Beck. *A Field Guide to Methodist Fresh Expressions.* (p. 40).

[50] Published in 1765.

[51] Yrigoyen, C. 1996. *'John Wesley: Holiness of Heart and Life'* (Nashville: Abingdon Press). Glossary.

[52] Maddox, R. 1994. *Responsible Grace: John Wesley's Practical Theology* (Nashville: Abingdon Press). (p. 83).

53 Clarke, A. 1823. *Memoirs of the Wesley Family: Collected Principally from Original Documents, Volume 1.* (London: J&T Clarke). (p. 94).

54 Carder. 2016. *A Wesleyan Understanding of Grace.* (Online). https://www.resourceumc.org/en/content/a-wesleyan-understanding-of-grace

55 In John Wesley's sermon, *'The Scripture Way of Salvation.'*

56 John Wesley, from his journal.

57 Ibid.

58 Heath and Scott, *Longing for Spring: A new vision for Wesleyan Community.* (p.41).

59 Maddox, R. *Responsible Grace: John Wesley's Practical Theology.* (p. 83).

60 Ibid, p. 19.

61 Beck. *A Field Guide to Methodist Fresh Expressions.* (p. 94).

62 Yancey. *What's So Amazing About Grace.* (p. 269).

63 Explored in 'Called to Love and Praise.'

64 (Online). https://www.methodist.org.uk/our-work/our-work-in-britain/evangelism-growth/explore-the-god-for-all-strategy/ (accessed 30/5/23).

65 McIntyre, D. 2014. *Having Your Cake and Eating It: Wesley and the 'Third Way.'* (Online). (https://um-insight.net/perspectives/having-your-cake-and-eating-it%3A-wesley-and-the/). (accessed 30/5/23).

66 Beck. *A Field Guide to Methodist Fresh Expressions. (*p. 94).

67 Watson, D. L. 1998. *Class Leaders: 'Recovering a Tradition'* (Eugene: Wipf and Stock Publishers). (p. 23).

68 Percy, M. 2004. Contributing to *Unmasking Methodist Theology* (London: Continuum Books). (p. 210).

[69] Atkins, M. 2010. *Discipleship and The People Called Methodists.* (Online). https://www.methodist.org.uk/downloads/pubs-intra-discipleship-120710.pdf (p. 17).

[70] Methodist Church in Britain. 2017. *The Gift of Connexionalism in the 21st Century* https://www.methodist.org.uk/downloads/conf-2017-37-The-Gift-of-Connexionalism-in-the-21st-Century.pdf (para. 4).

[71] Sweet. *The Greatest Story Never Told.* (p. 76).

[72] Methodist Church in Britain. *Called to Love and Praise.* (Para. 4.7.9).

[73] Methodist Church in Britain. *The Gift of Connexionalism in the 21st Century.* (Online). https://www.methodist.org.uk/downloads/conf-2017-37-The-Gift-of-Connexionalism-in-the-21st-Century.pdf (para. 5).

[74] I readily acknowledge the need for caution in doing this, because this is only one way to view the value of the 'gift of Connexionalism' but I hope that viewing things this way round offers some fresh insights and imagination.

[75] Other paint companies are available!

[76] (Online). https://www.crownpaints.co.uk/inspiration (accessed 21/5/21).

[77] Brafman, O. & Beckstrom, R. 2006. *The Starfish and the Spider: The Unstoppable Power of Leaderless Organizations.* (London: Penguin Books). (Online).

 https://www.amazon.co.uk/Starfish-Spider-Unstoppable-Leaderless-Organizations/dp/1591841836

[78] Atkins, M. 2011. *Contemporary Methodism: a discipleship movement shaped for mission [The General Secretary's Report]* (https://www.baildonmethodists.org/wp-content/uploads/2011/05/02-The-general-secretarys-report-0511.pdf 2011) (paras. 20 & 21).

[79] Beck. *Deep Roots, Wild Branches.* (p. 12).

[80] Davies, R. 1963. *Methodism.* (London: Penguin Books). (pp 11-12).

[81] Hirsch, A. 2016. *Forgotten Ways: Reactivating the Missional Church,* (Grand Rapids: Brazos Press). (pp. 59-60).

[82] Wesley, J. *Sermon 61: The Mystery of Iniquity.*

[83] https://freshexpressions.org.uk

[84] Romans 8:28, NRSV.

[85] Hirsch, A & Ferguson, D. 2011. *On the Verge: A Journey into the Apostolic Future of the Church* (Grand Rapids: Zondervan). (p. 35).

[86] https://www.methodist.org.uk/our-work/our-work-in-britain/evangelism-growth/ (accessed 30/5/23).

[87] Bosch, D. Quoted by Hirsch in *Forgotten Ways: Reactivating the Missional Church. (p. 41).*

[88] Bevans, S. & Schroeder, R. 2004. *Constants in Context: a Theology of Mission for Today.* (New York: Orbis Books). (p. 7).

[89] Beck, *A Field Guide to Methodist Fresh Expressions.* (p. 157).

[90] Moltmann, Jurgen. 1993. *The Church in the Power of the Spirit: A Contribution to Messianic Ecclesiology* (Minneapolis: Fortress). (p. 107).

[91] https://strategiesforinfluence.com/peter-drucker-coaching-tips/ (accessed 30/5/23).

[92] Campolo, A. 1990. *The Kingdom of God is a Party: God's Radical Plan for His Family.* (Cleveland: Word Publishing).

[93] Snyder, H. *Church Business or Kingdom Business.* (Online). https://seedbed.com/church-business-or-kingdom-business/ (accessed 30/5/23).

[94] Beck. *A Field Guide to Methodist Fresh Expressions.* (p. 157).

[95] Ibid, pp. xv/xvi.

96 Ibid, p. xxiii.

97 Chilcote, P. 2004. *Recapturing the Wesley's Vision.* (Downers Grove IL: IVP Bookers). (p. 55).

98 Meadows, P. 2019. *The Spirit of Methodism: Missionary Zeal and the Gift of an Evangelist.* (The Asbury Journal). (Online). https://place.asburyseminary.edu/cgi/viewcontent.cgi?article=2456&context=asburyjournal (accessed 30/5/23).

99 Cameron, H. 2018. *Living in the Gaze of God*, (London: SCM Press). (p. 114).

100 Pocock, C. 2015. *The Origins, Development and Significance of the Circuit in Wesleyan and Primitive Methodism in England 1740-1914.* (PhD thesis, University of Nottingham). (p. 15).

101 Methodist Church in Britain. *The Nature of Oversight: Leadership, Management and Governance in the Methodist Church in Great Britain.* *(*Online). (https://www.google.com/url?sa=t&rct=j&q=&esrc=s&source=web&cd=&ved=2ahUKEwiZrbyHkKD_AhUaSMAKHepHDJwQFnoECBAQAQ&url=https%3A%2F%2Fwww.methodist.org.uk%2Fdownloads%2Fco_05_natureofoversight_0805.doc&usg=AOvVaw3dm7JloNZ_5A9EKQXz6hg0 2005) par 2.19. (accessed 30/5/23).

102 Atkins. *Discipleship and the people called Methodists.* (p. 11).

103 *A Fresh Expression of our Mission, Methodist Church in Ireland, Faith and Order Committee.* (https://www.irishmethodist.org/sites/default/files/Fresh%20Expression%20of%20Mission%20Draft.pdf p.5. (Accessed on 11/05/2021)

104 Sweet. *The Greatest Story Never Told. (*p. 79).

105 Atkins. *Discipleship and the People Called Methodists.* (p. 16).

106 Hunter, G. 1994. Cited in James C Logan, ed. *Theology and Evangelism in the Wesleyan Heritage* (Nashville: Kingwood Books). (p. 159).

[107] Bevins, W. 2019. *Marks of a Movement.* (Grand Rapids: Zondervan) (p. 121).

[108] Grundy, M. 2015. Multi-Congregation Ministry. (London: Canterbury Press) pp 56-58. Here, Grundy references Roland Allen, missionary to China in the early twentieth century, who powerfully argues of the need for local indigenous leadership to have missional and discipling effectiveness within different cultural contexts.

[109] Pocock. *The origins, development and significance of the circuit in Wesleyan and primitive Methodism in England 1740-1914.* (p. 10).

[110] Methodist Church in Britain. *The Nature of Oversight.* (p. 1).

[111] Ibid para 2.3. For some exploration of the significance of 'covenant.'

[112] Beck. *A Field Guide to Methodist Fresh Expressions.* (p. 158).

[113] Atkins. *Discipleship and the People Called Methodists.* (pp. 12-13).

[114] Ibid, p. 13.

[115] Methodist Church in Britain. 2008. *The Ministry of the People of God*, (Online). https://www.methodist.org.uk/media/2063/fo-statement-the-ministry-of-the-people-of-god-1988.pdf (para. 54). (accessed 30/5/23).

[116] https://methodistheritagetour.wordpress.com/2015/04/11/the-class-meeting/ (accessed 30/5/23).

[117] Standing, R. & Goodliff, P. 2020. *Episkope: The Theory and Practice of Translocal Oversight.* (London: SCM Press). This book explores the theme of 'translocal' episcope in some detail.

[118] *The Ministry of the People of God* (1988) recognises that this has become neglected — and yet was a vital part of early Methodist episcope. (Paras. 54 & 55).

[119] At the first Methodist Conference of 1744, when the question was proposed, "In what light are we to consider ourselves?" it was answered, "As extraordinary messengers, raised up to provoke the ordinary ones to jealousy."

[120] Despite — ironically — the embedded coding for this remaining in Standing Orders.

[121] Batty, M. 1988. *Stages in the Development and Control of Wesleyan Lay Leadership 1791-1878.* (Thesis for Degree of Doctor of Philosophy in the Faculty of Theology at the University of London) explores this in some detail.

[122] Reasons for the demise of the Class Meeting are also carefully and thoroughly explored by Andrew Goodhead (2010) in *A Crown and a Cross: The Rise, Development, and Decline of the Methodist Class Meeting in Eighteenth-Century England.* (London: Wipf and Stock).

[123] World Council of Churches. 1982. *Baptism, Eucharist and Ministry* (Online). https://www.anglicancommunion.org/media/102580/lima_document.pdf

[124] The communal aspect is also necessarily weakened by virtue of the role being so thoroughly diminished (apart from the Pastoral Committee.).

[125] This is all the more to be expected given the ecumenical models of Parish Priest and Vicar which so easily can be mirrored in any perceptions of Methodist presbyters.

[126] Standing Orders, however, still primarily refer to the presbyteral role in these distinctively Methodist ways.

[127] Croft, S. 2006. *The Future of the Parish System: Shaping the Church of England for the Twenty-First Century* (London: Church House). (p.78).

[128] Beck, *A Field Guide to Methodist Fresh Expressions.* (p. 41).

[129] *Called to Love and Praise.* (para. 4.7.1).

[130] *Called to Love and Praise. (*para. 4.7.11).

[131] *Called to Love and Praise.* (para. 4.7.10).

[132] Noted in *Celebration of Methodism in Stillingfleet*, May 2019.

[133] Tabraham, B. (Ed). 1995. *The Making of Methodism.* (London: Epworth Press). (p. 47).

[134] Methodist Church in Britain. 2008. *The Missional Nature of the Circuit* (Agenda of the Methodist Conference). (para. 5.4).

[135] Beck. *Deep roots, Wild Branches.* p. 8. Quoting National Director of Fresh Expressions US, Dr Chris Backert.

[136] Beck. *Deep Roots, Wild Branches.* (p. 85).

[137] Marsh, C. et al. 2004. *Unmasking Methodist Theology* (London: Continuum Books). (p. 209).

Printed in Great Britain
by Amazon